paula pryke flower school

paula pryke flower school

photography sian irvine

jacqui small

This book is dedicated to all the people who have attended our flower classes in the United Kingdom or been present at one of my many overseas or home demonstrations. Many have become regular visitors, making our flower school in London feel more of a club than a school. Several have gone on to become firm friends and in particular I would like to dedicate this book to my very dear flower soul mate Sybil Sylvester. Long may the magic of flowers continue to inspire and beguile us all!

First published in 2006 by
Jacqui Small LLP,
an imprint of Aurum Press Ltd,
7 Greenland Street, London NW1 OND
Text copyright © Paula Pryke 2006
Photography, design and layout copyright
© Jacqui Small 2006

Publisher Jacqui Small
Editorial Manager Kate John
Editor Sian Parkhouse
Flower Checker Susanna Longley
Designer Maggie Town
Production Peter Colley

A catalogue record for this book is available from the British Library.

ISBN 1 903221 37 4

2010   2009   2008   2007

10 9 8 7 6 5 4 3 2

Printed and bound in China

contents

introduction

Everything you need to know to arrange flowers in the Paula Pryke style can be found in this book, whether you wish to be a competent flower arranger or whether you are the serious student of floristry. Once you have learned the basics – the techniques and the elements of good floral design – you will be able to create any design you wish. When you have mastered these skills you can start to create your own style and in time become a serious floral artist. Designing with flowers has given me immense pleasure over many years and I feel very grateful to have found this vocation. Above all I hope that this book will spread the gospel: good floral design is enjoyable and rewarding for everyone – not least the floral designer!

Contemporary floristry has developed enormously over the last four decades and new styles are constantly emerging and gaining prominence. The industry is becoming a much more integral part of modern design and is led by architecture, art, interior design and fashion. Within each of the main continents there are distinct styles and influences and for the last thirty years it would seem that Europe has been the major focus of attention for new styles. One of the main reasons why the standard has been so high in Continental Europe is that generally there has been a greater regard for the importance of professional training. Generally this means that before someone opens up a floristry business they have had some formal training and apprenticeship. It is far more common in Europe to find that a florist is an accredited Master florist who has learned his or her craft as a full-time student of floristry and has served some apprenticeship with another professional before starting their own business. In these European countries you are far less likely to have anyone start up a flower shop and call him or herself a 'Designer Florist!' without any formal training because the competition is so strong. At the moment anyone can

start a flower business and in the United Kingdom, and in some other parts of the world such as the United States, it is relatively easy to set up in business. Lots of people have a very romantic view of the flower industry and think that working with flowers will be the panacea for life. They set up a business before they have fully mastered the basic skills or at worst are not even aware that they have huge gaps in their floristry and business knowledge. I have to confess that I changed careers and 'fast-tracked' my study of floristry. At the time I was lucky that the flower industry in London was not very developed and lacked any media profile. My fresh approach to flower arranging and the artistic way the shop was laid out immediately attracted many clients and the media's interest. At the same time several other designers opened shops and businesses in London and before long we were all competing for work in the same market place. This pushed up the standard of floristry, and now in hindsight I can see I was at the start of this revolution in floristry in this country. At the time I was too busy working and trying to make the business profitable to notice!

Northern Continental Europe has also produced some very impressive florists, particularly from Sweden,

Denmark, Norway, Austria and Switzerland. The style of German floristry has always been very strong and certain florists have tirelessly spread their unique talents throughout the world, such as Gregor Lersch, by lecturing and demonstrating worldwide as well as teaching in his native Germany at his base in Bad Neuenahr. As the Netherlands has such supremacy in the world flower market it is not very surprising to discover that they too have many fine florists and have been very prominent in moving forward the professionalism of the flower industry. The Flower Council of Holland has helped to promote good design as well as flower marketing. Marcel Wolterick is my favourite Dutch contemporary, whose sumptuous designs make the most of the individual flowers. Belgium has spawned some very talented florists, with Daniel Ost being the most well known internationally. The style for the Belgians and French is generally more romantic and flowery than in the more northern parts of Europe, and one of my favourite florists is Christian Tortu, whose natural fresh style always delights me. Many of these talented people, through increased

international travel and the new media, have impacted on floristry style worldwide. Emerging interest in floristry is now coming from China, Vietnam, Thailand as well as lots of South American countries. There is also an interesting merge of Eastern and Western floral design, with the strong influence of Ikebana permeating European design and many Japanese students moving from Ikebana to European design.

In the UK we have always had a deep interest and passion in gardening and this spawned florists who worked initially with the big houses and their lavish gardens and later in the bespoke nurseries. The occupational florist and flower shopkeeper emerged in the twentieth century. Floristry is the term given to the world of the professional florist who earns a living from working with the natural plant world. Flower arranging was the domain of the lady at home who was usually an amateur and who enjoyed arranging flowers either for the Church or in flower clubs. Very often these amateur flower arrangers would join a club and exhibit or compete with other flower arrangers. The garden was an important source of plant material and generally

they had no commercial side to their hobby. Over the past ten years this distinction has blurred, and more people are turning a hobby into a business at the same time that there is more commercial interest in the flower industry. Department stores, supermarkets and petrol stations are marketing flowers, and Internet companies sell direct from the growers. More and more flowers are being sold on the street by market stalls and the variety of people involved with the flower industry has mushroomed enormously.

I started my own floristry career by training at the famous Constance Spry School for floristry. I then went on to study for a traditional professional floristry course at a vocational college in London and worked as an apprentice to a London florist. I immersed myself in floristry and flowers and devoured every book I could find on the subject. I visited many shops to access the market place, wholesalers and garden centres to broaden my knowledge. After three years of working part time in a flower shop and cramming myself with information I took the plunge and rather naively opened my own flower shop. My fresh and natural new style hit London at a time when British floristry was sadly lacking in flair. However, within a few years of opening my shop there emerged a group of new floral designers, many of whom, like myself, had come from other career directions, and soon we were competing for work and raising the standard of floristry first in the capital and then throughout the United Kingdom. Just three years after I began my business I was approached to write my first book and it was at this point that I realised that I had established a unique new style of floral design.

Paula Pryke

I feel strongly that the role of a florist is to artistically interpret the ideas and requests of his or her clients with plant material. At one level this could be a hugely creative art form, making giant decorative structures that command an immense budget for plant material, or, at completely the other end of the spectrum – but no less worthy – creating a simple tied bunch of flowers as a 'thank you' gesture, or artistically wrapping a simple stem as a tribute for a memorial service. It is only occasionally that we have the opportunity to be completely and unrestrainedly creative and innovative and design solely for our own satisfaction. This may be in our own homes, for a competition or when we are working on new collections of personal floristry work. Whether designing for ourselves or for others, over a period of time we create our own style.

my signature style

Massed monochromatic flowers are a favourite of mine, not least since massing is one design style that looks very effective both in informal and formal situations. I most often use all one type of massed flower or monochromatic arrangements in my own home where the strength of colour in the arrangement highlights a room. The use of one colour throughout a party theme or decorating an event creates a very dramatic look, particularly when using tall-stemmed glass containers, as pictured here. These are perfect for filling huge ballrooms with flowers with dramatic effect while allowing seated guests at each table to see each other and talk across the table. Here, the large headed 'Clooney' ranunculus are mixed with the gorgeous black 'Queen of the Night' tulips, 'Extase' and 'Grand Prix' roses with a few deep red peonies. Trails of ivy had been placed across the tall red Martini-style glass vase to give rhythm to the arrangement and to make it look more natural.

RIGHT The development of the widespread production of these tall thin glass vases, ranging from 60 cm to 120 cm, has been immensely influential on the decoration of ballrooms across the world. Simple but effective, this look is created by arranging layers of scrunched-up cellophane and petals, to which water is then added. The vase is topped with a tightly-packed hand-tied arrangement of orange 'Wow', green 'Jade', lilac 'Coolwater', red 'Passion' and burgundy 'Black Baccara' roses.

Some of these ideas have been re-visited over the years and have become very much a part of my own signature style. The flowers may change as new varieties appear, the style of vase may alter and the colourways are amended quite dramatically, but the essential design remains.

PREVIOUS PAGES Vanda orchid and lilac skeletonised leaf has been wired onto a pearlised elasticised bracelet. I discovered these bracelets in the United States, where florists are often asked to make wrist corsages for the end-of-school 'Prom'.

A large round summer hand-tied bouquet has been placed in one of our signature-style box carriers. This 'just picked from the English garden border' look is one of my favourites. It includes peonies, dahlias, and 'Blue Pacific' and 'Sterling Silver' roses mixed with stocks, agapanthus and mint, *Viburnum tinus* berries and *Alchemilla mollis*. It has been wrapped in Deconet and then aqua packed for safe transportation.

For a long time I had admired the very decorative gateaux designs that were a signature style of the Copenhagen florist Tage Anderson. Then, during a visit to a large floral relay corporation in the United States, I discovered that a rather mundane cake flower design had become the rage and was one of their best-selling items. When I returned home, I created my own version of the birthday cake and this now has become a perennial favourite of our design range. The base is made from rosemary, although heather works equally well, and normally I use roses because they have a uniform head size; however, it can work just as well with small round-headed summer flowers such as cornflowers, margarite daises and asters. Among the pink roses used here are 'Illusion', 'Beauty By Oger', 'Esperance', 'Sweet Akito' and the green rose, 'Jade'.

The topiary candelabra looks particularly good against a blank canvas and is perfect for marquee or tent wedding venues. Using flowers in season always creates the best and most emotional response from the observer, and once you have the metal frame you can add whatever seasonal decoration you like. In spring I add blossom, in summer, ivy and in winter, dried or painted twigs or heavily berried branches. The base of the candelabra has been covered with wet floral foam and moss. A round 30-cm wreath frame has been placed on the branches of the candelabra so that flowers can be added to the top. Wired around the metal frame are birch twigs with sprouting catkins and moss, to which lots of spring jasmine and ivy has been added. The frame has been highlighted with lots of lilac blossom and purple lisianthus and groups of 'Blue Pacific' roses. The stunning effect of cascading informality befits the romantic ambiance that candlelight imbues.

These designs are massed with lots of flowers and foliage, giving a colourful textural impact. They are inspired by a love of the English cottage garden look.

ABOVE Using a simple design and repeating the idea is very effective and it makes more visual impact. This trend has been a very popular theme in recent years, either using the same mixed selections of one flower or using just one type of flower. Rather than the flowers being grouped in arrangement, it is the containers that are displayed together. Here, mixed sweet peas have been hand tied and displayed in matching frosted glass vases.

RIGHT A perennially favourite colour combination is pink, lilac and lime green. This spiralled hand-tied bouquet of pink astilbe, cerise 'Milano' roses, dahlias, peonies, hydrangea, and double purple lisianthus is made more vibrant by using the lime green foliages of fountain grass and *Viburnum opulus*. The spiky 'Green Revert' chrysanthemum has a slightly less acidic tone than the shamrock chrysanthemum that is often used.

This cube glass vase is so versatile and allows you to create many different feels within it. Here equisetum stems have been used in a uniform way to hide the green floral foam and this combination of red 'Grand Prix' roses and green cymbidium orchids with burgundy roses is one of our most popular designs for Valentine's Day. For most of my designs, a third of the plant material is foliage, and as a general rule, I try to select three different types to add texture. Here ivy berries blend with red skimmia and hebe.

I often go the fruit and vegetable
market for inspiration, particularly in
winter when the flower choice is more limited.
I am particularly fond of the glaucous colour and feel
of the Savoy cabbage. I have been using Savoy
cabbages as a basis for an arrangement for well over a
decade. I core out the centre and fit a polystyrene cup
filled with floral foam. They look best filled with roses and
here 'Milano', 'Wow' and 'Grand Prix' have been arranged
in the foam with a touch of red skimmia. Savoy cabbages
look great sprayed gold or silver and filled with red or
white roses respectively for the festive season.

RIGHT Flower trends closely follow fashion and when striped fabric was all the rage, soon enough we were creating very geometric flower arrangements. Perspex has been very popular as a container as it can be easily made up to any size or colour desired. Originally, the idea for this design came from designing a party with a black and white theme where I used white 'Akito' and 'Black Baccara' roses in low oriental-style black dishes. The floral foam can be concealed with a raft of either straight twigs or reeds such as the natural equisetum. The foam is also concealed by bright pink gravel and rather than a chequer-board effect, this arrangement was created using diagonal lines of pink roses – working from the left, these are 'Dolce Vita', 'Aqua', 'Milano', 'Pink Renate', 'Poison' and 'Milano'.

OPPOSITE This twiggy basket with glycerined oak leaves has been wired onto a sturdy basket. I use a supplier in Spain who makes some exquisite baskets and I found ones that also combine 1-cm chicken wire, useful for building into structures like this or using to attach fruit. To this basket I have added some sumata wood, which is new to the floral market and is very much in demand. This sumata wood, which is usually more popular for continental or oriental designs, has been 'flocked' to give it a furry coloured coat. Here I have used brown, but I have seen it in the most vibrant shades of blue, lime green, red and pink, as well as black. Into the basket I have snugly fitted a glass vase filled with water packed around with moss. The roses, which include 'Beauty By Oger', 'Halloween' and 'Aroma' roses are mixed with miniature pink anthuriums. The dark red skimmia and a few brown rudbeckia heads bring the brown of the base through the arrangement.

LEFT This lavender basket has been in popular demand for June weddings for over ten years. There is something completely divine in being able to fashion the base out of this wonderful scented flower. The small bunches of lavender have been tied with raffia to the basket and the interior has been packed with moss. A plastic bowl filled with floral foam has been added to the top and filled with scented mint, blackberries, *Alchemilla mollis* and masses of garden roses. This organic style works surprisingly well in modern interiors as well as rustic settings.

Classical topiary shapes always look good and over the year it has become a trademark to use flowers and fruits or vegetables. This has the added advantage of giving great texture to the design and it also can be better commercially as very often fruits and vegetables can also be considerably less expensive than flowers to purchase. Here I have chosen aubergines because of their colour and shiny texture. They are also quite firm and so are perfect for wiring into a moss frame. When choosing the flowers for a dense arrangement like this, it is advisable to use some larger headed flowers or foliage to help cover the expanse. Here, ornamental cabbages make the perfect filler. Camellia leaves and skimmia also form the base with 'Aqua' and 'Avalanche' roses predominating the design. Pussy willow has been added along the contours of the design to give a more natural feel.

This arrangement started out as a design for a wedding where the bridegroom unusually was organising the flowers as his bride was overseas. My brief from the client was for a large round arrangement that included candles and that was low enough so that you could see across the table. When he also asked me to combine his favourite flowers, the tall birds of paradise, I had to go back to the workroom and try out a few sample ideas before coming up with this design. The birds of paradise were placed in a pin holder in the centre of a straight-sided 30-cm glass dish. Water and floating candles were added. Around the edge of the dish I fixed a 35-cm floral foam ring, which was edged in galax leaves, and the base was greened with coral fern and *Viburnum tinus* berries. The South African foliages *Leucadendron* 'Safari Sunset' and 'Silver Brunia' were added for texture and visual interest. Groups of the brightly coloured pink 'Milano', orange 'Wow' and pinky orange 'Milva' roses were placed around the ring. The orange of the strelitzia was picked out with the textural leucospermum and the purple was emphasised by groups of the double purple lisianthus. Bright pink 'Serena' gerberas and short gloriosa flower heads completed the vibrant ring. The eye is brought from the base to the heads of the birds by using a few branches of contorted willow.

ABOVE Natural clay pots are always a winning container for flowers and I am always drawn to old containers such as these oil pots from Provence. I have quite a collection of these and this is one of my largest which I have filled with foxgloves and coral and red peonies, mixed with dark purple *Prunus* and the dangly explosions of fountain grass. The grass softens the arrangement and the flowers and foliage are in harmony with the vase. Frequently I find that this kind of classic arrangement will suit traditional spaces and soften more contemporary interiors.

RIGHT For a long time I have been buying inexpensive lampshades as covers for vases for big events. I was first attracted to the lampshade when I found some being made from horizontal rings of ribbon by a local designer. These made such a perfect companion to the mixed flower posies that after that I often sought the lampshade department for inspiration. Here black satin shades have been filled with the large-headed burgundy 'Clooney' ranunculus and red peonies. The drama of the arrangement has been completed by using a ring of black feather boa. When the whole thing is encircled by small red nightlights it makes a very dramatic and romantic table centrepiece.

These simple arrangements are often the ones that stand the test of time. New floral 'fads' come and go but simple blocks of colour always look good. These bow vases filled with one type and colour of flower still look good fifteen years after the idea was first mooted.

These bow vases have remained one of my favourite vases for nearly two decades. They are very beautifully coloured hand-made glass vases by the artist Paul Williams. I used a set linked together for my second book and the photograph went on to become a very long-standing poster by a famous worldwide Swedish furniture maker. These muted spring colours have been diagonally spaced, starting with yellow ranunculus, deep blue hydrangea, lime green 'Shamrock' chrysanthemums, deep blue hyacinths and pale yellow 'Winterburg' tulips.

LEFT Sometimes clients leave the design and plant choices to me, giving me artistic license! Very often these have been times when new designs have emerged. This fishbowl arrangement was created for a charity competition among designers at the London flower market. It won first prize and it has been one of my most imitated designs. 'Mango' calla lilies have been arranged with orange leucospermums in a bed of green berries from Thailand.

OPPOSITE This design was originally a collaboration with two of my designers, Anita Everard and Rachel Mashiter. Rare white spathiphyllum flowers from Holland have been teamed with pussy willow to make a round cage. Set in a low frosted dish with floral foam concealed by white sand, the pussy willow has been shaped into a ball. The spathiphyllums have been placed in the foam and are bound onto the frame with silver aluminium wire. Adding a few blocks of glass ice completes this icy white look. I particularly like this design with green 'Midori' or 'Pistache' anthuriums.

BELOW I love boat-shaped containers for long dining room tables and this is one of two I have by one of my favourite accessory companies, the Dutch firm DKHOME. The starkness of the black and silver lacquered vase is complemented by spray-painting some contorted hazel silver and placing it through the fresh flower design. This delicate arrangement uses phalaenopsis orchids, eucharist lilies, white peonies and double-headed peach hollyhocks to add a touch of pretty colour.

part one

fundamentals

British *Vogue* once described me as 'anarchic' and when describing my work, journalists will often say that I break all the rules. Before you can find your own floral style you need to be grounded in many of the fundamentals, as they are the structure, the mechanics and the method you need to know in order to be creative. As floristry is a living art form – which is most often also commercial – flower arrangers and florists need to understand and execute the basics to be able to move on artistically.

design rules

In short, you cannot really begin to break the rules until you know what the rules are. Although a lot of my arrangements are very simple in essence and some do break 'perceived wisdom' on flower designing, I would always recommend any wannabe florist to learn all the basics and to study design work of many different florists from all over the world to gain a very broad view of the profession. Personally, I would like to see the standard of the profession ever rising, so whether you are charging for your services or not, it is your duty to present your designs in an imaginative yet competent and secure way, which is why you need to know and understand the fundamentals.

Good floral design in my opinion should be immediately attractive and appear effortless and natural – in other words, take a group of flowers and foliage that are individually appealing and create a composition that enhances their beauty. I can appreciate the work of many floral designers whose style and methods are quite different from my own, but it is my own personal conviction that the flowers should be the stars of the design and that the design should never be allowed to overpower the natural beauty of the flowers.

It is quite difficult to analyse the elements of good design in any art form, but basic design principles can be applied to all forms of art. In floral art a good design not only combines these design elements in its construction, but it also takes into consideration such factors as the occasion and the setting for which the flowers are intended, the purpose of the design, and the budget of the patron. Indeed, the *raison-d'etre* of any flower arrangement is the starting point for any floral designer. Flowers are always sent, given or displayed to convey personal messages or to create an ambiance. The floral designer has to have empathy with their client to be able to use the flowers appropriately to set the desired scene, or to convey the right emotion. Effective floral design has to marry all these elements, ensuring that the material, the design and the location are all harmonious and on budget!

The floral foam ring is immensely useful for decorative floristry. Here a 35-cm frame has been used to create an arrangment with two levels of interest. The base is full of textural flowers such as bluey green hydrangea, dracaena leaves, flowering eucalptus and eryngium. Groups of three 'Grand Prix' and 'Coolwater' roses are placed at different heights and levels around the ring. Four purple pillar candles are wired into the frame and nine tall purple 'French' tulips are placed around the ring in three groups placed in a natural vegetative way.

shape and form

There are three factors that underlie all good floral composition: form, colour and function. There is an enormous diversity of shapes, form and patterns in the plant world and some study of flowers, plants and trees in their natural habitat will be invaluable for creating good floral design. Before I became addicted to floral design, I was in love with nature and spent most my early childhood enjoying the outdoor life in my home county of Suffolk, England. The organic world has been a powerful source of inspiration to artists of all disciplines throughout history and, in my opinion, many forms in nature are the best shapes to emulate. The shape of a tree, the structure of plants, individual flower heads, grasses, leaf and flower patterns – they are all inspirational for new designs.

In my floral work I like using styles which take a very holistic approach and display the flowers as if they were growing. This works particularly well for arrangements on windows or mantelpieces or even small landscapes on tables. These designs are very suitable for informal arrangements with a wildflower feel. I have also found much inspiration from the garden vegetable patch or trips to fruit and vegetable markets, and incorporate cabbages and cauliflowers frequently in my work. Most floral designs will feature a number of different attractive forms displayed together.

Hundreds of different shapes and forms of flower arrangements (but not all) have clear-cut definitions or easy descriptions. However, there are some everyday designs which will be the first shapes and forms you will learn to make. First, you need to decide whether the arrangement you wish to create will be round or front facing. Round arrangements can be viewed from all sides while front-facing ones will normally be displayed against a wall or on a mantel so that all of the interest is concentrated on one side.

Making the vase part of the arrangement has been a trademark of mine since I began floristry and every year there are new styles of vases to arouse our creativity. The widespread arrival of a very light aluminium wire available in many bright colours as well as metallic bronze, silver and gold inspired this new design, in which orchids can be suspended throughout the vase. A hand-tied arrangement of pink phalaenopsis orchids, edged with anthurium leaves and bound by more aluminium wire, tops the vase.

The next decision will be whether you wish to create a formal or informal arrangement. Do you want something with strict geometric lines or something loose and free flowing? Sometimes it may be easier to create a loose natural display than a more formal one. However, creating a successful informal arrangement can be much harder than making a very geometric formal arrangement.

mass style
This is the first of the two main arrangement forms in floral design, where there is little space in the arrangement, such as a dome of roses or a tightly arranged topiary. The mass style has its origins in Europe and is often considered very English. Inspiration for this type of work may have been drawn from early still life paintings, particularly the work of the 17th-century Flemish and Dutch painters. The Victorians especially loved the formal style of mass arrangements and they designed and created many silver vases to hold their displays. It is currently more fashionable to use this style of arrangement in a much more loose and informal way.

Within the massed style there are many different forms. It could be a simple bunch of mixed flowers in a vase or a dome of one type of flower, such as a tulip or ranunculus. These massed displays are generally known as 'posy' or 'domed'. Traditionally, these were also referred to as 'Biedermeier' designs and originally consisted of concentric circles of flowers with a collar of foliage.

The traditional massed arrangement can be made using either foam or chicken wire and can encompass small and large designs; from an arrangement for a small alcove to a trailing mantelpiece or pedestal arrangement. In most cases, this style has an upright axis that relies on line material. Dominant focal flowers are added, before finishing with filler material for an overall massed effect.

This massed topiary is a popular form and has been created by cementing a birch pole into a plastic pot and then spray-painting it silver. The plastic pot is placed in a glass cylinder and then concealed by layers of brightly coloured aggregate. A floral foam ball has been taped and wired securely on the top. A base of flowering eucalyptus, skimmia and ivy berries have been added all around the foam ball, and a selection of gerberas in shades of pink massed over the top.

LEFT The Victorian posy – where massed flowers are placed in concentric circles – is a classic design and one that traditionally was often wired together. This one has been hand tied by working circles around a central rose. Widow iris, blue muscari, and white narcissus follow, after which the posy is edged with massed violets.

It is also possible to make hand-tied bouquets in the line style and I tend to sell more of this design as 'masculine' hand-tied arrangements, intended for male recipients. I believe the line style shows off architectural flowers such as strelitzias, agapanthus and other tropical flowers to their best advantage. I can understand why it is more popular in countries where more colourful flowers such as these grow, and also where there are fewer herbaceous flowers.

Within the line form there are many different styles. The most common is the architectural vertical arrangement. As I have already noted, the Japanese style of Ikebana also falls under this style.

line-mass
This style of arrangement uses flowers in larger massed groups, and it was in the 1950s and 1960s that this style of work became very popular. Constance Spry and Julia Clements pioneered flower arrangements and popularised arranging flowers in the home as an artistically satisfying experience. It was also in the 1950s that floral foam was invented, allowing amateur flower arrangers the opportunity to create a more structured arrangement; hence, popularity for line-mass arrangements was, in some way, dictated by the new mechanics that became available at the time. Currently, the line-mass style is much more popular than the straightforward line arrangement.

Within the spectrum of the line-mass style there are many forms of flower arrangements which one can create and, in some ways, the early teachers prescribed a code which has been slavishly reproduced to this day. Although one has to learn some rules, this so-called code for flower arranging has been regarded by some as too stifling and rigid, and many feel it is responsible for producing flower arrangements that are not very visually

Massed flower heads may also be used in topiaries. This ancient art form originated in Eastern Europe and the cone-shaped topiaries are often known as Byzantine. The shape is either fashioned by moss or foam and the flowers, leaves, and sometimes fruits, are pinned or placed in the moss or foam. The use of moss allows the designer to mould any shape. This technique is suitable for very large arrangements for special events where the life of the arrangement is usually quite short.

line form
The line form style is usually a formal arrangement using tall flowers and structural plant material. There is far more open space and only part of the shape is filled with flowers and foliages. This style of arrangement originated from the East, most notably China and Japan. It is not known precisely when the line style was adopted in the West, but the first Japanese Ikebana arrangements are recorded as being shown at the Chelsea Flower Show in London in 1912, and it was sometime in the 1950s that the Americans started to take an interest in the Eastern style, with line arrangement reaching a peak in the mid 1970s.

pleasing. There are many designs that fall into this category and it is necessary for any student of floristry to be aware of them.

the symmetrical triangle One of the most popular line-mass arrangements which, in my opinion, is one of the least attractive.

the asymmetrical triangle This can be a useful arrangement to create at either end of a mantelpiece, but I would almost always veer towards a massed asymmetrical arrangement.

the crescent shape This is a moon-shaped design that is normally constructed in a shallow dish. A clever choice of plant material is required for this design to be successful, and it is a testing choice of arrangement for any student to make well.

the Hogarth curve So called because the artist William Hogarth described an elongated 'S' as a line of beauty. This is an interesting shape in and of itself, and with the right plant material it can be visually pleasing.

parallel style This is a style which has been very influenced by European floristry, in which the mechanics generally include a rectangular block of foam set in a shallow dish, from which groups arise vertically. I like this style when the designer tries to make the arrangement as natural as possible, but am less in favour of very structured versions. This is an interesting technique that is generally more important in competitive floristry than in the wider commercial world.

the deconstructed style A recent fashion in floral design, this involves taking a number of vases collected together either to display one flower head or a group of flowers. In its most extreme form, this style can be a way of

using petals to construct a flower or a design; for example, using flower heads to create a lei or a daisy chain. It takes some inspiration from Asian cultures and their traditions in flower arranging.

Many of my designs would be classed as unconventional or free style – they do not fit any particular category and they are not bound by any rules of design. They are often inspired by fashion, art, architecture and design and are very popular currently. Contained arrangements are also in vogue, where all rules about the size of the container in relation to the arrangement are abandoned and the flowers are used inside a glass vase.

BELOW The current trend in floral design is for deconstructed arrangements. This is an example of where the arrangement is actually in the vase and almost the antithesis of perceived floristry rules. The Victorians were crazy about terrariums, indoor glass gardens and artificial flowers in huge glass domes. In the 1970s bottle gardens were all the rage and now the manufacture of huge glass vases has created the vogue for arrangements of cut flowers within the vase. Here eight yellow calla lilies have been arrangemd with three small monstera leaves.

LEFT Into this square container a structure of kiwi vine has been created, providing a frame through which some flexi grass has been woven. 'Cognac' anthuriums have been added following the flow of the kiwi vine, resulting in a lovely light and well-balanced arrangement.

balance

Balance in flower arranging is about physical balance and visual balance. Physical balance is obviously very important when creating an arrangement to keep the whole thing stable, particularly when creating a large pedestal or mantelpiece arrangement for a special event. Poorly constructed arrangements can topple over and be a danger. Whether you are using foam or a vase or even creating a hand-tied bouquet, you need to make sure that the plant material is placed to spread the weight over the entire area of design.

Studying nature can help enormously in understanding visual balance. Regard the density of a group of reeds growing together, take inspiration from the scale of a stem of a flag iris in relation to its bloom, enjoy the patterns of magnolia blossom in early spring. By using nature as your guide, you will be able to create beautifully balanced arrangements.

Visual balance is more complicated to explain. In general, the eye is drawn to the area in a design that is perceived to contain the most interest. The materials in a visually balanced design will be arranged around an imaginary vertical or horizontal axis so the eye is drawn equally to both sides. Using equal amounts of flowers may create symmetry or make a design look rigid; as a guide, choose darker flowers, which look heavier than pale ones, or use round flowers that look heavier than trumpet shapes. In a large design, tall delphiniums and digitalis can be visually balanced by trailing amaranthus or ivy over the edge of the base of the design. The movement created by the foliage counter-balances the strong linear flowers, adding texture and softness. The incorrect placement of plant material will make a design look unbalanced or at worst unattractive or even ugly.

This tall thin vase
arrangement has actual
balance so that the weight
of the fritillarias are equally
weighted to make the vase
stable. The willow gives
more visual balance to the
overall look and the collar of
lilac hydrangea gives
stability both in real terms
and also visually.

harmony

Harmony is a hard concept to describe and a quality that is in some ways intensely personal. A harmonious arrangement is one that is artistically pleasing and where all the natural elements of the design work together well. It is the quality I look for when accessing the work of a floral designer of a very different style from my own. A harmonious result is achieved when balance, scale, repetition, rhythm and proportion all effectively work together. In other words, none of the design rules should conflict. The most useful way to understand harmony is to look at combinations of materials

When selecting flowers and foliages for a vase, focus on the colour and proportion of the flowers, to give a pleasing shape with a good outline and a natural feel. This harmonious vase combines seasonal flowers in greens, pinks and lilac and includes a good mix of shapes such as the tall delphiniums, the round 'Shamrock' chrysanthemums and peony tulips, with lilac and guelder rose to fill. Light tendrils and buds of lisianthus lighten the outline while the solomon's seal creates a soft edge between arrangement and vase.

as they are found in nature. For example, if you created a spring woodland scene using a combination of moss, bark, cowslips, violets and primroses, the harmonious balance would be lost by adding a commercially grown rose.

A fresh bunch of cow parsley in an earthenware jug displayed in a rural cottage is in harmony to its surroundings. Often the simplest and most uncontrived arrangements are the most successful in achieving overall harmony. Too much variety of plant material, overuse of accessories and overworked designs are apt to confuse and often destroy the effect of harmony.

The brown, green and sandy shades of these pulses has been matched by the hand-tied posy at the top, which includes peonies, dahlias, fountain grass, hydrangea, *Alchemilla mollis* and green dill. The base looks rustic and is in harmony with the flower choice.

There are many occasions where the simplicity of using all-white cut flowers looks absolutely stunning. I particularly like to use white with a minimum of green so the effect is more arresting. I also love to use white flowers in frosted vases to give a very clean feel to the design. Here 25 heads of white phalaenopsis orchid have been hand tied with three small monsteria leaves and then placed in an elegant frosted vase. The proportion of the spray of these delicate flowers perfectly complements the elegantly tall vase.

scale and proportion

For an arrangement to be in good proportion, there needs to be the right mix of elements, whereby the plant materials need to relate well and both the dimensions and quantities of the design should be in proper scale with the chosen surroundings. Proportion is also a vital consideration for choosing both the container and the flower. For centuries, in fact ever since the foundations for good proportion were laid down by the Ancient Greeks, a formula has been established which has been considered as a pleasing proportion. The golden 'section' or 'ration' suggests that proportion should be

about 1:6 and over time this led to flower design rules being laid down which suggest that the flowers would be 1½ times the height of the container. Although this benchmark may still be considered for competitive flower arranging I think that this formula, which was originally applied to the proportions of the human body and which fundamentally was applied to architecture, cannot be rigidly applied to an organic art form such as floral design. It is more theoretically interesting than practical. Certainly, it allows designers to create classical design of great proportion, but it is

BELOW This very classical arrangement of greenery and creams includes gardenia foliage, guelder roses, lilac and 'Avalanche' and 'Alexis' roses. These grouped flowers are in perfect proportion to the silver bowl as they are around 1½ times higher than the container. You develop a sense of proportion and balance as you progress with your flower arranging skills – getting the proportion wrong a few times is usually the fastest way to learn good proportion!

ABOVE It is very important that the flowers chosen are in perfect scale to the vase, so for this miniature urn I have chosen to use the dimunitive snake's head fritillarias. I am often asked which comes first – the container or the flowers – and generally I prefer to take my inspiration from the flowers and then decide on the container.

applies equally to the interior space for which it is intended. A large white space will suit a bold arrangement. Similarly, a dark panelled room will require an equally bold statement in order to compete with the interior.

While adopting these general principles for proportion, some designers like the challenge of creating large designs from flowers and plants of tiny proportions. Small plants or flowers heads are then massed and placed in tall structures. The most commonly used and popular arrangements of this type is one in which the mass of proportions is upright. Examples of upward proportions include large classical pedestal arrangements, most vase arrangements, line arrangements and parallel, natural and vegetative arrangements.

In my own work I am fond of the upright proportions but, since I like my arrangements to be quite natural, my upright arrangements are asymmetrical and weighted in proportion by trailing foliages and flowers. I love very droopy arrangements where the emphasis of the proportion is downward, and where the greenery and flowers cascade in a waterfall effect. Several arrangements command this look, among them are the trailing arrangement above a fireplace and the droopy low arrangement that is traditionally positioned at the front of the bride and groom's table at a wedding reception. For a less happy occasion I use flower designs with downward proportions when creating a spray to place on the top of a coffin which also trail over the sides.

Horizontal proportion is often used for low table arrangements, side tables or for corporate work. This is far more popular in designer floristry than in the everyday bread-and-butter work of a florist. When a designer creates a ball or spherical shape he or she is creating an arrangement of symmetrical proportion. The density of the plant material is uniform, so visually it has the same proportion through the entirety of the shape.

too rigid for the inspirational floral designer. It also takes no account of the constant change in fashion and also the different ways that most of today's top floral designers create their own organic containers.

Whichever way you approach the design, the flowers, the foliage and the container all have to be in proportion to the design. Usually the space determines the overall size of the arrangement and then a suitable container is chosen. With this established, the designer then chooses plant materials that are in proportion to the container and the desired size of the arrangement. This is important both in terms of the size and scale of the flowers as well as their colour. Some colours may dominate the flower choice and also change the visual proportion of the arrangement; this

For larger classical arrangements it is important to use tall and large headed flowers to keep the arrangement in proportion to the vase or, in this case, urn. Large star-haped cream 'Concordia' lilies with tall branches of forsythia and foxgloves give height. Huge heads of hydrangea, coral peonies and chrysanthmums make a good impact and look appropriate in the sturdy verdigris urn. The fountain grass and cream hypericum provide a soft edge around the urn and add downward proportion.

texture and contrast

Putting a group of flowers together with the same textures and creating a bunch or a tightly packed area gives enormous impact to any kind of design and is favoured in contemporary floristry. The grouping of plant material of the same colour and type in tight groups is also sometimes referred to as blocking. Next to colour, texture is one of the most important decisions when putting together a group of flowers for any design. I love to create patchworks or blocks of texture and when planning a list for purchasing flowers at the market, I always try to include as many textures as I can to give the composition depth. I usually achieve this even in very inexpensive arrangements by using at least three different types of foliage, with five being my preferred

number. Plant material comes in lots of different textures: some flowers and leaves are glossy, such as bright red 'Tropical' anthuriums and waxy green monstera leaves. Some almost have the texture of fabric: the heads of celosia look almost like woven chenille and are available in many gorgeous colours; the texture and pattern on the leaves of the *Anthurium crystallinum* is quite astounding and can be so dominant in a design that it dictates a strong choice of accompanying flowers to complement its own strong form and texture.

One textural favourite of mine is the pincushion protea *Leucopsernum cordifolio*, which pops up again and again in my work and designs. I love the contrast of its spiky and furry flowers against the deep, velvety texture of

BELOW This ring is full of textures, from the soft and furry leucospermums to the velvety 'Circus' and 'Cherry Brandy' roses. The lotus seed heads have lovely markings almost like shower heads, while some of the foliage is shiny, such as the galax leaves and the folded aspidistra. The berries of the 'Red Flair' hypericum are bright and glossy and the guelder rose and white skimmia with their small florets give the ring some lightness and movement. The elegant 'Mango' callas and the flexigrass give the dense foliage contrast and add richness and impact to the overall design.

roses, or next to the dense flower heads of the gerbera daisy. Prickly flowers such as the artichoke flower *Cynara scolymus* need strong flowers to complement their striking and strong character. Fluffy or feathery flowers such as gypsophilia or the South African *Serruria florida* need to be mixed with strong regular shapes, such as roses or carnations.

Contrast refers to the different effect created when two pieces of plant material are placed next to one another. Sometimes a design requires a diversity of plant material. A large round classic pedestal for a celebration requires contrasting forms of flowers, for example, round shapes, star shapes and spires,

mixed with contrasting foliage. A contrast of texture is achieved when one piece of plant material is of a different density to the one placed next to it. A shiny surface is more compelling to the eye than a rough texture. This is particularly useful when creating designs with a monochromatic theme. The different colours, shades and tints of plant material can also be used to create a striking contrast. Being placed next to a matt leaf or branch will enhance any bright flower. I love to create contrast in my designs and therefore deliberately choose to use contrasting colours and textures; very often the result is a rich and dramatic arrangement.

ABOVE The delicate white flowers of eucharis and jasmine in this simple hand-tied bouquet contrasts with some hebe, *Garrya elliptica* and one of my favourite textural foliages, *Senecio greyii*. By contrasting the delicate against the dense, you often create a surprisingly arresting result.

movement

A good-looking design uses techniques and materials that move the eye from one part of the display to the next. When there is rhythm in the design there is movement to the eye, allowing the arrangement to appear natural and alive. Without movement, an arrangement can look static, artificial and unattractive. There are some accepted ways of getting movement into an arrangement, one of which is to use some curved and natural looking stems and plant material. Choose various sized blooms so the flower head size is not too regular. As a rule, use at least three different types of foliage, preferably five, and ensure they are of contrasting sizes and shapes and include at least one with texture such as blossom or

berries. It is a good idea to choose flowers at various stages in their development. Spray flowers such as roses or lisianthus enhance a sense of movement. When you place the plant material, make sure you use some to recede into the arrangement as well as placing some on the outer extremities of the design. Try to hide all straight stems which may make the arrangement look rigid.

The effect of movement is created through the use of line and colour in the design and by executing repetition or graduation. This principle gives flow to the arrangement and encourages the eye to move along and through the container. Here, the trailing shape of the pink phalaenopsis orchids and dyed vine give movement to a contemporary arrangement in a simple vase.

dominance

Cymbidium orchids would normally be most dominant in an arrangement because they are large, have many heads, and are visually very arresting. The use of the folded pandanus leaves subordinates the orchids, changing the visual dominance within the overall arrangement.

In most arrangements, with the exception of round arrangements, there is an area of dominance that is known as the focal point, centre of growth or centre of interest. It is the area of the arrangement to which the eye is drawn. Traditionally, there was only one area of dominance because too many competing dominant areas of one arrangement can be confusing to the eye. Usually the focal point is a choice flower or group of flowers or the area from which all the stems appear to radiate. In contemporary floristry, a number of attractive alternatives have evolved, providing many diverse areas where the eye may be drawn and where there may be several points of interest. These focal points may be below the container in a trailing arrangement, in the container of a horizontal arrangement, or way above the container of a standing bouquet.

The phormium leaves weaving throughout this long, low horizontal design take the eye through the composition and out to the peach tulips.

rhythm

Rhythm in music gives a composition its feeling and flow, and also stimulates the visual senses and imagination. It is exactly the same for a flower arrangement. Rhythm gives movement to a design, making it more pleasing to the eye. The perceived rhythm can come from the progression of one flower or one type of foliage throughout the arrangement. This flower or foliage creates a strong visual line. Rhythm gives excitement to an arrangement, which may otherwise look solid or fragmented. Three other elements can add rhythm:

1   Repetition of a group of flowers or of a design. Repetition is one of my favourite devices for this and can be achieved by using groupings of materials in an arrangement or groupings of the same arrangement. Usually the same type of flower or colour is grouped together to create the repetition of an idea. This immediately enhances the single design.

2   Transitional flowers and foliages are important to the study of rhythm because they complement the lines of the design and allow the eye to travel easily from one part of the design to the other. Flower size and colour play an important part in achieving good transition. A great arrangement allows the transition from one piece of plant material to the next to occur as unobtrusively as possible.

3   The plant material should all radiate from a central point of the growth. This gives the arrangement elegance and grace and makes the rhythm of the design look natural.

ABOVE I love this boat-shaped container: the arched pussy willow has been prised into the two ends of the boat to fit snugly and cymbidium orchid heads have been arranged along the length. The eye is drawn naturally across the willow from one flower head to another.

Colour blocking has always been an important visual look for the commercial florist and can look very effective in a hotel foyer as well as for a celebration. Three red glass tear vases have been topped with round floral foam balls decorated with small gerbera daises know as 'Germini'. These chunky arrangements are made visually more attractive by the design being repeated. Odd numbers of designs work better than even ones, particularly with symmetrical designs like these.

repetition

The repeating of elements in floral design, currently very popular in contemporary floristry, creates a feeling of movement, and adds colour and textural interest to the design, giving it stronger visual impact. Today there is a vogue to repeat a simple design by placing one, two, three or even more identical arrangements together. This incredibly simple idea may comprise something as simple as the placement of stems in a group – it is the repetition that gives the groups visual strength. Thirty bubble vases placed together with one marguerite daisy in each is more arresting that one vase with thirty stems. A group of narcissus arranged as living topiaries looks stunning down the centre of a long table or across a mantle. Also currently very fashionable is to use the repetition of colour by placing three or five or even more glass vases together and massing one variety in one colour in each vase.

ABOVE Two very simple vase arrangements are grouped together for more visual impact. Each vase has a bunch of Iranian dogwood, one cymbidium orchid and one monstera leaf. The visual lines are repeated and the plant material looks more impressive in two vases than it would in one. As these arrangements are very asymmetrical they look fine arranged in odd numbers.

Bunches of violets have
been edged with wired and
skeletonised lilac leaves
and then bound together
to create this small
textural massed posy.

massing flowers

Floral designs in which a mass of one material is used with very little space have been popular at different times throughout floristry history and flowers have always been massed by florists to create funeral tribute work, when the massing of heads together allows the florist to create shapes and letters. However, the widespread massing of flowers for all types of arrangements and celebrations is now very popular with flower arrangers all over the world. The impact is very immediate as there is a mass of colour and texture. The individual line or form is not seen, only the mass of flowers. Massed flowers can take the form of an arrangement in foam, such as the posy pad pictured below left, or on an oasis ball like the gerberas below right. Alternatively, they can be hand tied, as in the vase arrangement pictured opposite or wired as in the rose and ivy posy pictured right. Whatever the methodology, the visual impact is very strong, and at some point, all types of florists, however different their styles, will use massed flowers.

ABOVE Twenty 'Iceberg' roses have been hand tied into a domed posy and then edged with trails of variegated ivy to soften the edge of the vase.

FAR LEFT A posy pad has been edged with galax leaves and then massed chrysanthemum heads have been placed in the soaked floral foam. The floral tribute has been topped with a spray of 'Black Baccara' roses with forget-me-nots, lilac and sweet peas.

LEFT A round bowl has been filled with bright pink aluminium wire and topped with a large floral foam ball massed with pink 'Serena' gerberas to form a massed table centrepiece.

grouping

Grouping flowers is perhaps the single most important technique for creating contemporary arrangements. Rather than mix a group of flowers through an arrangement, they are placed in groups, which creates a stronger visual flower arrangement. In classical work, flowers are often grouped to create a greater visual mass or for prompting a focal point. Grouped flowers may also be used in topiary shapes, whether round or spherical.

The contemporary practice has been led by the desire to use diverse and unusual colour collections. Grouping flowers lets you use colours that would be visually unpleasing in more traditional, scattered arrangements. In a

grouped arrangement you can place greenery or a complementary colour next to one group of flowers so that you create peace between colours that do not usually look good together. I like the device of using dark coloured flowers such as black and burgundy and placing them next to brightly coloured flowers such as magenta, orange and lime to achieve really colourful designs. The key is the nature of the balance; it is not necessary to always group in odd numbers but do make sure there is great visual balance. Working with groups suits my own style of design as I love pushing back the boundaries of traditional colour sense and because, quite simply, I love bright colours.

BELOW I have chosen to contrast the pale peach 'Toscana' rose with the dark burgundy 'Black Baccara' rose. The almost black dracaena leaf which covers the bowl and the black ivy berries help to enhance the groupings of the colours. White lilac, lime-green guelder roses, and cymbidium orchids are used in equal balance to create a rich texture. This unusual colour combination is visually enhanced by the tight groupings.

This is a very classic urn table arrangement using glossy green camellia foliage with groups of 'Avalanche' and 'Alexis' roses, mixed with white lilac, lime-green guelder roses and white 'Diamond' bouvardia.

bunching and bundling

Bunching involves taking a group of the same variety of flowers and placing them together to create one unit. The bunches can then be placed in an arrangement with ribbon or raffia, or wired into a design. This bunching is also a textural device and can create more interest in an arrangement where there is a limited choice of floral material. It is also very suitable for very short flowers such as snowdrops and violets, which can then be pinned into a design. Bunching has its traditions in the English country house style where lavender, wheat, and barley were often used, and is still commonly used for dried flower arrangements. Generally, plant material chosen for bunching is long lasting and can exist without water for a while, which is why twigs and cinnamon are popular, or long-lasting foliage such as bamboo or equisetum. In late summer, late harvested lavender or wheat can be used which will then dry out naturally.

Bundling is the term given to tying together a number of stems for ornamental effect. Sometimes bundling can make use of a waste product like the end of stems or smaller lengths of material which have been disregarded for a design. For example, I often bundle up cinnamon sticks to use in winter flower arrangements. Bunches of dogwood or equisetum also create an interesting effect in a winter design. The tie itself can also add colour to the arrangement, so that if you wish to add a bright colour you can incorporate an appropriate tie in coloured wire or fabric. If you want the bundling to look as natural as possible raffia or grass may be used.

BELOW LEFT Bundling is the design technique in which quantities of material are firmly bound together to create a pattern above the binding point and sometimes below. A sheaf of wheat is an example of a bundle in which stems radiate above the binding point and also below. Here these lovely pink calla lilies have been bunched together to create two areas of interest above the binding point of bright pink aluminium wire. This simple bunched design would be a stylish contemporary bridal bouquet worn with a simple wedding gown or may also work in an elegant vase.

RIGHT Binding or wiring several of the same plant materials together and wiring them into an arrangement is a technique traditionally used for garlands. Many wood carvings that date back to the Elizabethan period depict early forms of this bunching. This technique is more likely to be used in midsummer when there are lots of seed heads and herbs around or in midwinter when making garlands using either cinnamon sticks or groups of dried and sprayed bunches of twigs. Here fresh lavender has been bunched into a swag with wired fennel bulbs to create a lovely natural garden feel. Green and white hydrangea and blowsy garden roses are grouped on a base of *Viburnum tinus* berries.

carpeting

This technique is most often used to create low table centrepiece designs or as a base for more vertical placements, when it is sometimes known as the groundwork. Variations of textures are used to create very short stems of plant material. Patterns of lines are crafted using moss, twigs, textural foliages and flower heads. Carpeting can afford some variations in height, but I prefer this style when it is low and tactile, like a collage. This floristry technique is used more in winter when plant material is less available or when a florist wants to set a theme.

pave This is a term borrowed from jewellery designers, and refers to the use of setting stones close together so that no metal is visible. In floristry, paving refers to covering the surface of a design or an object such as a sphere with a mass of plant material so that it creates a uniform area with little variation of depth. The most common application of this technique is to cover spherical balls with bun moss or chrysanthemums such as the tiny uniform 'Santini' varieties. The effect of such plant material is to create a flat 'cobblestone' surface. The materials chosen for this can be floral and freshly cut or dried. Leaves, fruit, pods, berries, vegetables, mosses, pulses, and even stones are used. Fresh flowers and foliage are usually arranged into green floral foam, whereas dried material may be pinned or wired or occasionally glued.

BELOW This very contemporary table centrepiece uses the heavy contrast of the diagonally cut cigar reeds *Cannomois virgata* against the very delicate cappuccino-specked pink ranunculus and balls of fluffy green *Viburnum opulus*.

layering

This technique is by no means a new one in floristry and was originally used as far back as ancient Egypt. Layering flowers, leaves and fruit is still popular in many cultures. In Hawaii it is customary to thread flowers to create leis. In

southern Europe, bay leaves are threaded onto string to dry out, and in South America, chillies are threaded in rows to dry. Today, the most commonly used layering technique uses overlapping leaves to hide the wire. Some floral artists use glue to stick the leaves but I am rather averse to the glue gun, only getting it out for the festive season or when all other methods have failed. My preference is to use double-sided tape to layer leaves onto containers to create sculptural containers. Traditionally, layering was used to create military decorations, and it is now used most notably in sympathy work to make floral chaplets. It now has a wider audience due to themed parties and the demand for more sculptural pieces, which are often designed for large event work.

ABOVE This garland of carnation heads and galaxy leaves has been strung onto a heavy florist wire. The wire goes into the top of the stem and through the ovary of the flower and out through the top of the corolla, onto which the next flower or leaf is strung, creating a layered effect.

LEFT This floral foam heart topped with roses has been edged with layered glossy camellia leaves. They have been placed slightly on top of each other so that they create a layered effect, giving depth and movement to the pinned leaves. Most often one leaf is laid on top of the next to conceal the pinning.

manipulating plant material

Winding arrangements became fashionable at the end of the twentieth century, and like many trends, they were adopted with a passion. Starting with natural materials, the technique then progressed to accessories until everything became wrapped up and constricted! You have to have a certain temperament to be good at this kind of work, because it is very time consuming. It is also more relevant to specialised floral design than everyday work because of the labour costs in creating these pieces.

leaf weaving & manipulation

There are many types of plant material that lend themselves to be woven or bent to enhance a display. I was first fascinated by this art of leaf weaving and manipulation on a trip to Thailand and have since incorporated it in simple ways in my own designs. Galax, ivy, aspidistra, aralia, flax, and grasses, in particular, steel, lily and flexigrass, are all suitable plant materials. Equisetum has very graphic lines and is one of the most commonly used. The Victorians nicknamed the aspidistra plant 'the cast iron plant' and it is one of my favourites for bending around the end of hand-tied bouquets or for concealing containers. It is inexpensive, long lasting and very durable. It can be bent or the stem can be used to pierce the leaf to form a curve. Round leaves such as bergenia or galax can be formed into a cone shape or roll. Sculptural forms can be made by plaiting palms such as areca or kentia, but this form of manipulation is best left to the experts.

BELOW My favourite aspidistra leaf has been bent around a small collection of bright pink peonies, gloriosa and *Viburnum opulus*. These leaves are inexpensive and create a lovely collar for a few flowers, making it seem a far more extravagant and gorgeous bouquet. The organza ribbon bow is one of my own, which I use especially for Valentine's Day. It has the lovely Goethe inscription: 'The flower is a leaf made with love!'

This design was first created for the 40th birthday party of a New Zealander who wanted to use native phormium in her party decorations. The New Zealand flax is extremely versatile and lasts very well, so it has been used for numerous weddings and parties, but it is also a favourite for our corporate work. Here, the pink 'Telstar' amaryllis have been supported internally by a bamboo garden cane which helps the hollow stems hold the weight of the heavily hybridised head and also keeps the stems firmly anchored in the foam. Bun moss has been pinned onto the floral foam to hide the mechanics of the arrangement.

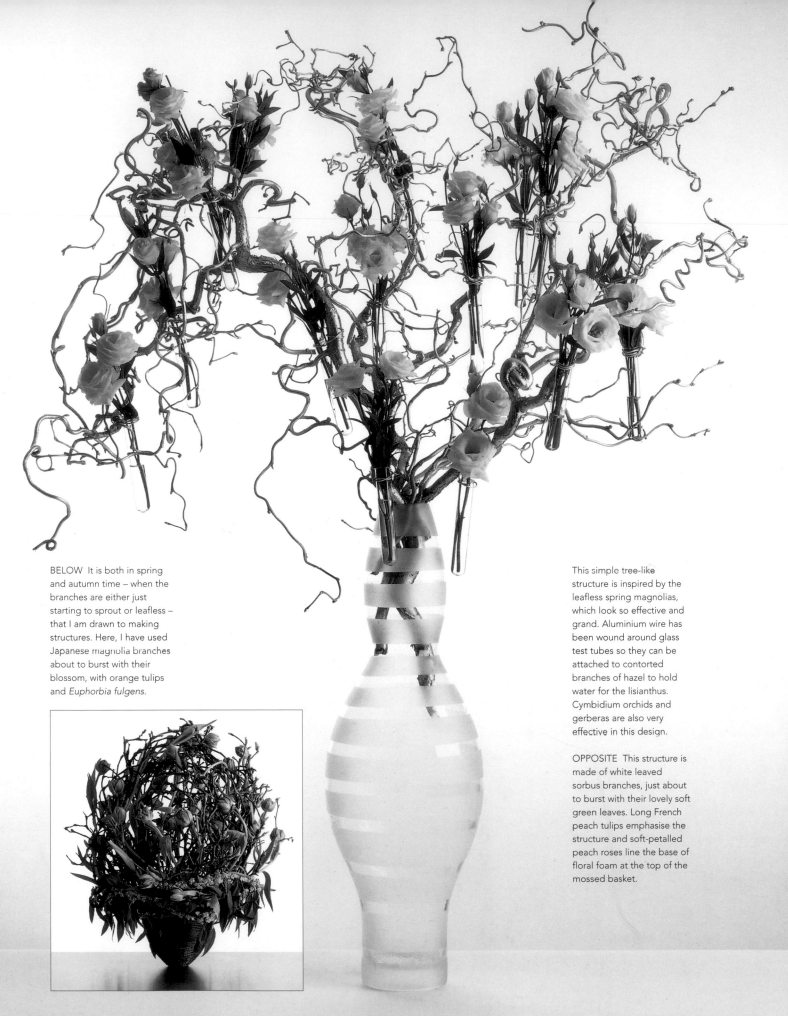

BELOW It is both in spring and autumn time – when the branches are either just starting to sprout or leafless – that I am drawn to making structures. Here, I have used Japanese magnolia branches about to burst with their blossom, with orange tulips and *Euphorbia fulgens*.

This simple tree-like structure is inspired by the leafless spring magnolias, which look so effective and grand. Aluminium wire has been wound around glass test tubes so they can be attached to contorted branches of hazel to hold water for the lisianthus. Cymbidium orchids and gerberas are also very effective in this design.

OPPOSITE This structure is made of white leaved sorbus branches, just about to burst with their lovely soft green leaves. Long French peach tulips emphasise the structure and soft-petalled peach roses line the base of floral foam at the top of the mossed basket.

structural designing

Flower structures are created by tying, twisting, threading and wedging. Creating structure from plant material has become increasing popular over the last twenty-five years; this is a time-consuming and complex way to arrange flowers and has great popularity among competitive floristry. This includes bending and even clamping plant material. Raffia, string or wire are used to secure these natural frames together. Shallow containers, organic-looking pots or glass are ideal vehicles for structural designs. Often the container may be completely concealed by plant material.

Some structures are decorative and some are used as mechanics. For example, a grid of dogwood over a vase can be used as mechanics for an arrangement. A cage can be constructed to contain flowers. Plant material with pliable stems is popular for these kinds of constructions, such as willow, trailing rose, eucalyptus, kerria, and vines such as honeysuckle, jasmine, clematis and kiwi. Tough trailing greenery such as passion flower, jasmine, ivy, smilax, ferns and ruscus, and dried sticks and reeds, such as thin mikado sticks, are also very efffective for this type of work.

This style of floristry is too fiddly and labor intensive for both my patience and my design aesthetic, but there are elements that I do use. Many of the principles can be applied to more everyday floristry and even to hand-tied bouquets. The ball of pussy willow and spathiphyllum on page 29 and the magnolia opposite are structures which have been designed to draw the eye into the centre of the arrangement and to emphasise the beauty of the plant material used for the construction. Willow is very supple when the sap is rising in the spring and falling in the winter, so this plant material leads you to work during these seasonal times. Japanese magnolia flowers before the leaf appears, so it is particularly attractive to work with in the spring.

season

The wide selection of flowers available to today's consumer is largely unseasonal, with the top sellers distributing flowers such as roses, chrysanthemums, carnations and alstromeria across the world. Being largely cultivated and heavily hybridised, they are available all year round with absolutely no discernible 'best' season. However, for the flower arranger and the florist, there is still a wealth of seasonal produce; from the first clutch of English snowdrops, to the exquisite scent of narcissus from the Channel Isles or the first few bunches of mimosa from Italy.

It is also the seasonal change within foliage types that hugely influences floral design. In spring, the leafless branches sprout into action and in autumn, colourful foliages arouse new designs. The full leaf foliages in midsummer encourage more classical full-blown style arrangements, and the limitations on flowers in the winter motivate designs based on evergreens. As the year unfolds there is a seasonally rich palette of colour and texture.

For this spring arrangement a collar of contorted willow has been fashioned by twisting together lengths into a wreath frame. Designed to sit on the edge of a frosted vase, it enhances the magnificent seasonal crown imperials.

OPPOSITE FAR LEFT This early summer arrangement is constructed by using a hand-tied posy of yellow and red achillea, strawberry-red godetia, variegated mint, lime-green *Alchemilla mollis* and *Viburnum opulus*, with sprigs of rosemary and garden roses. It has been placed on top of a glass bowl filled with fruit and water.

OPPOSITE LEFT This cube arrangement is one of my most versatile designs and can be made in any seasonal style. For this autumnal vase we have lined a block of floral foam with red dogwood and then filled it with red skimmia and rosehips, groups of ruby red roses and 'Alexis' roses and cymbidium orchids.

Traditionally, these forced amaryllis bulbs are a favourite around Christmas, but these statuesque beauties are having their seasons extended each year because of their immense popularity as a long-lasting cut flower as well as an interesting indoor bulb. Here these winter white amaryllis have been arranged with leafless Japanese magnolia into a glass vase filled with floral foam concealed by sand and delicate coral fern.

colour concepts

There are dozens of reasons why I feel so lucky to have enjoyed a career working with flowers, but by far the single most joyful experience has been working each day with this immense choice and variety of colour. Colour is my inspiration and it has a very powerful psychological effect on our state of mind. The colour of nature is simply about attracting the attention of birds, insects and animals for the pollination and fertilisation of the plant kingdom. This very essential and sensual process in the plant world has always led to a close association between the natural plant colour and human activity and has been an extremely enriching bond.

I think it is fair to say that some florists and flower arrangers have a very natural flair for using colour and they have an almost instinctual understanding of it. For many others, the use of colour and the immense choice at their disposal is daunting and so it is necessary to have some basis of understanding of the theory of colour. Over the next few pages I outline some of the theory of colour although I have written more extensively about this subject in my seventh book, *Living Colour*.

As a florist I understand the need to use colour effectively to make an attractive arrangement and very often to convey a feeling or emotion on behalf of our client. Professional florists must work with the colour preferences of their clients and, as most gift flowers are sent to convey an emotion since colour plays an essential role in producing the desired result. When clients are ordering flowers they more often talk of colour than varieties of flowers or even their budget. Colour is very often the first thing on our client's mind.

My favourite flowers – pink ranunculus – have been mixed with pink astrantia, rosy pink 'Sandy Femma' roses and lime green balls of *Asclepias physocarpa* 'Moby Dick'. Dyed pink coconut fibre and artificial butterflies give extra colour to the overall flamboyant combination.

Although white is not technically a colour, more the absence of it, in the plant world it offers several colour combinations. This living topiary is made of seven white amaryllis tied beneath their flower heads and at the base of their stems, arranged in a frosted glass vase with a collar of white lilac. The choice of a white container reinforces the monochromatic harmony of this design.

harmonious colours

A colour harmony is created when a group of specific hues are placed together. There are three primary colours: red, yellow and blue. By mixing these you create the secondary colours of green, violet and orange. Intermediate colours are created when a primary and a secondary are mixed. The glaucous blue green of the Savoy cabbage or hosta leaves is an intermediate colour. The red-violet found in the dahlia and tulip families is another example of intermediate colour. The 12 colours are known as hues, representing the names of the colours from which they were created: yellow, yellow-green, green, blue-green, blue, blue-violet, violet, red-violet, red, red-orange, orange and yellow-orange.

The intensity of colour is the degree of saturation that the colour projects. A fully saturated colour such as brilliant red is more intense than a maroon or burgundy. If you try to imagine colours in black and white you can understand this further. A pale yellow is nearer to white whereas a very dark brown is nearer to black. The perceived value of each colour, how pure it looks, is relative to its position to black and white. Navy blue is lower in value because it is closer to black. Colours are lightened by the addition of white, muted by the addition of grey and dulled by adding black.

Changing the value of a hue by adding white, grey or black produces a tint, tone or shade. By altering the value of a hue, an artist controls the effect or the emotion produced and stimulated. Mother Nature produces a diverse range of colour and it is the skill of the floral designer to combine this wonderful offering into a carefully orchestrated harmony of hues, tints, shades and tones!

When one colour is used to create harmony it is known as monochromatic harmony. Often this produces the most subtle and pleasing of combinations and consists of a single hue in variations of tints, tones and shades.

BELOW In true colour theory the use of green with red would not be considered a true monochromatic colour harmony, but, since everything in the plant world includes some green it is unavoidable in floristry colour theory. Equisetum has been attached with double-sided tape and tied with sea grass to a glass tumbler, into which a small posy of senecio, skimmia, 'Passion' roses and red anemones have been placed.

RIGHT A hand-tied bouquet of deep red peonies, red skimmia, lime-green guelder rose, variegated deep red carnations and stems of flowering rhubarb has been arranged into rings of rhubarb in this early summer arrangement.

BELOW Rosemary has been arranged around a glass tumbler onto double-sided tape and tied securely with sea grass and a spring posy of ivy berries, senecio, narcissi, muscari and pink ranunculus has been placed inside.

complementary colours

Using complementary colours is a good starting point for selecting flowers. They conform to our perceived thoughts on what good colour combinations are and this appeals to most people. Colour in floral design has to be viewed from two perspectives. First, is the relationship of one colour to another in the composition. This is expressed by the colours chosen and by their relationship in scale and size to one another in the design. To make a combination 'look' complementary you need to balance the colours fairly evenly. The second perspective is the relationship of colour to the design. The colours must reinforce the design and the effect you wish to achieve.

A complementary colour harmony is the combination of any two colours which lie directly across from one another on the colour wheel. Green and red are opposite and so are blue and orange and purple and yellow. These are known as complementary colours. When they are formed by using hues either side of the colour wheel they are referred to as split complementary colours. Pale pink and lime green is one such split complementary colour combination. The truest direct complementary combination on this page is the red and green but because lime green is more of a hue then it also veers towards a split complementary. The pale pink, blue and grey combination is visually complementary (although not strictly theoretically) because all the hues are very similar in their intensity. The colour wheel theory is useful for an understanding of colour and its relationship with other colours but you will find that it soon becomes quite instinctual as to what works well and looks good, and what jars the eye and is not so pleasing.

Cut limes conceal floral
foam into which pink
bouvardia, white lilac, pink
calla lilies, pink 'Beauty by
Oger' roses and pink
cymbidium orchids on a
base of *Viburnum tinus* and
ivy berry foliage have been
arranged. Flowering
Viburnum tinus has been
used for the base, with
some lime green balls of
guelder rose to carry
the lime green of the
fruited base through the
pink arrangement.

This brightly coloured ring of yellow and pink mixed with purple is essentially an analogous colour combination. The pink and yellow gerberas have been interspersed with groups of 'Grand Prix' roses, orange leucospermums, purple double lisianthus and the short stemmed gloriosa. Fitted onto a pin holder in the centre are five tall red heliconias.

mixed colours

Any colour can be made to work with another colour provided it is in the right balance and has the correct amount of foliage to create a foil for the colour and texture. Being confident in mixing colours comes with experience and each new season brings new hybrids and fresh colour combinations with which to experiment. In nature many different colour mixes totally defy any serious 'colour theory', often within the same flower or plant! A clutch of multi-coloured wildflowers can often inspire an idea for a colour scheme that I may not have considered. Sometimes an individual variety can suggest a new colour scheme. A good colour combination enhances the beauty of the individual flower by placing it with other colours. Creams and whites are very enhanced by lime greens. Yellow can be best in a monochromatic design but I like to mix it with blue, which sits opposite on the colour wheel and therefore makes it a split complementary colour, but I think it needs a lot of softening with foliage and texture to stop it from looking too 'corporate'. Cobalt blue delphiniums work very well next to huge late summer sunflowers with tall yellow eremerus, some pale yellow 'Concordia' lilies and a bunch of purple tracheliums and lisianthus. Soften it with some feathery yellow 'Dille' and you have a favourite yellow and blue combination.

BELOW Galax leaves have been used to line the inside of a stemmed glass bowl, which has then been filled with soaked foam, and a bed of asparagus foliage. Forget-me-nots, soft blue lilac, lime-green guelder roses, deep purple anemones, hot pink gloriosa and 'Milano' roses make this an analogous harmony of different colours.

RIGHT A frosted glass dish is filled with 13 'Vendelle' and 12 'Primadonna" roses and edged with dark green ivy trails around the base to conceal the floral foam.

analogous colours

Colours that are on either side of each other on the colour wheel are known as analogous colours. Generally speaking this is one of the most popular and acceptable ways of mixing colours and I have to say that it crops up time and again in my own work. I do not think about them as being analogous colours, but if I were to look back over most of the mixed coloured arrangements in my portfolios, the vast majority would fit into this category with the addition of greenery! Not all my arrangements, however, would fit into the strict 'colour theory' definition, which states that an analogous colour

combination should include one primary or secondary colour with adjacent colours on the colour wheel from a 90-degree angle. This is partly due to the constant addition of greenery, whatever the colour combination.

An analogous colour combination would suggests that they should be related. For example, yellow, yellow-orange and orange work well as do red, red-violet and violet and so on around the colour wheel. In most flower arrangements there is also the addition of the secondary colour green provided by the foliage, as a base for the colour.

This analogous colour combination takes in the lime, which is a yellow-green next to yellow on the colour wheel and, on the other side, yellow-orange. A plastic bowl is covered in double-sided tape and encircled with yellow broom into which two blocks of floral foam are added with a chunky arrangement of cream 'Alexis' roses, 'Yellow dot' spray roses, guelder rose, 'Daily Star' green chrysanthemums, white skimmia and some mixed sunflowers.

contrasting colours

Contrast is the difference shown when a variety of plant material is placed next to one other. As well as contrasting colour, texture and form are important in creating a good arrangement and whatever colours are chosen, they will both play an important part in achieving the overall look. Creating a good contrasting arrangement involves using the two colours on the outside of an analogous colour mix in greater balance to those inside the semi-circle. For example, blue and yellow are at the opposite ends of an analogous combination, so a more arresting colour combination comes from having more of the two primary colours and less of the dark green in the centre. It is the same with orange and green: they are at the ends of another analogous combination, so by using them without primary yellow in the middle you get a more striking combination.

Complementary colours which lie across from each other can often make the strongest contrast, and if you use two colours that are too close to one another you need to use texture to get a greater contrast. For example, strong textural contrasts are often needed to make monochromatic designs work.

BELOW Stripes of bright orange and lime green aquarium aggregate have been used to line a block of soaked floral foam in this 16-cm cube. Matching orange 'Wow' roses, bright orange germini gerberas and textural orange leucospermum have been contrasted with green ivy berries, 'Lemon and Lime' roses and 'Jade' hypericum.

Lilac hydrangea florets have been placed in a vase with layers of cellophane to create an iced water effect. A hand-tied bouquet consists of 'Daily Star' lime green chrysanthemums, 'Green planet' roses, lilac hydrangea heads, guelder rose, *Alchemilla mollis*, and 'Duchess de Nemo' roses. Lime green is a very special colour and I use it a lot to create a fresh and more vivid colour scheme, in a variety of combinations.

the effect of foliage

I use foliage to make colours tone together. Generally, I try to use at least three different types of foliage as that gives the finished design a more natural appearance. If you use the same group of flowers but add three types of foliage usually with one in blossom or with berries, depending on the season, you will get a much better looking design than if you choose just one type of foliage.

To make a combination brighter add more lime green; to tone it down use darker green glossy foliage. To perk colour up, lighten it by using foliage with more white, such the silver greys of eucalyptus or senecio. For more depth use foliage with more black in the colour – denser greens like huckleberry, camellia,

ruscus, ivy and aspidistra. Brown foliage adds depth; photina, leucadendron and cotinus with their lovely deep colours have more impact because of the contrast of the dark against the brightness of the flowers, so I often include these with my more unusual colour combinations.

Green is generally a neutral colour but lime green is the least neutral, adding zing and vitality to any arrangement. Traditional flower arrangers have long lusted after lime-green foliage such as moluccella, *Alchemilla mollis*, hellebores, euphorbias and hydrangea. The hybridisers know lime green is popular and each season brings lots of new varieties to add to the collection of old favourites.

Although some variegated foliage can be great for flower arranging, such as pittosporum and varieties of eleagnus, holly and ivy, I am very wary of variegation as it can introduce a lot of yellow or cream and detract from the other colours. I therefore only use variegated foliages in winter when there is less choice and I mix them with other evergreen foliages.

ABOVE This chunky bouquet of burgundy cotinus, lime-green leucadendron, pinky peach rose 'Toscani ', green 'Baubles' South African foliage, *Berzelia galpinii* and gardenia foliage is edged with anthurium.

LEFT A soft trailing wedding bouquet needs light foliage whereas a bold design needs dense foliage for structure and balance. Here 'Toscani' roses are mixed with *Asparagus densiflorus* 'Sprengeri', *Asparagus setaceus* 'Plumosus', *Clematis montana* and 'Gracia' spray roses.

LEFT White ranunculus and white parrot tulips have been mixed with glossy dark green foliage, ivy berries and aspidistra for a sophisticated hand-tied arrangement.

BELOW Using a lighter green selection of foliage, which here includes the white flowering skimmia, *Alchemilla mollis* and 'Jade' hypericum, gives the flowers a much more vibrant hue and overall a lighter visual effect.

part two

lessons

To be a successful florist and to forge your own style, you must first learn the basics and then it is essential to get lots of practical experience. It takes time to become a competent florist and a lot of this expertise is learned on the job. Throughout this section each lesson is broken down to teach you the basics of flower arranging and floristry. Starting with mastering a hand-tied bouquet, the lessons then progress to making arrangements in foam, and using a pin holder, chicken wire and even moss. Each stage is photographed to help you master the techniques and concepts required for arranging flowers in my style. Whether you are a veteran of the design workroom or new to the world of flowers there is always something new to learn and new trends and fashions to keep your work fresh and appealing.

essential equipment

In the floral industry the word 'mechanics' is given to describe the equipment necessary to keep the flowers in place. To start off with you only really need a good pair of scissors, a sharp knife and some strong secateurs. Next you will want to get hold of some wired string and some blocks of floral foam and pot tape to secure the floral foam. Changes in commercial floristry have meant a greater diversity of media is now being used with flowers, such as shells, fruits, vegetables, gravel and glass products such as donuts and test tubes, just to name a few.

You can buy floral sundries from either flower clubs or from sundries wholesalers. Most of these are attached to fresh flower markets. Some suppliers also sell these goods over the Internet. Buy yourself a sturdy workbox and gradually build up your sundries as you perfect your skills.

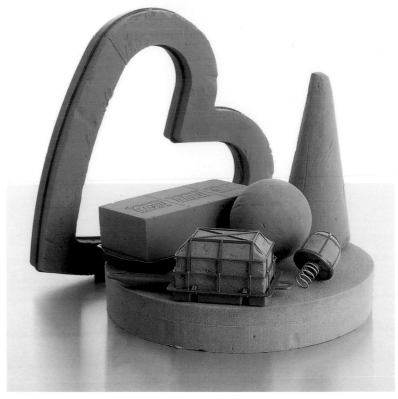

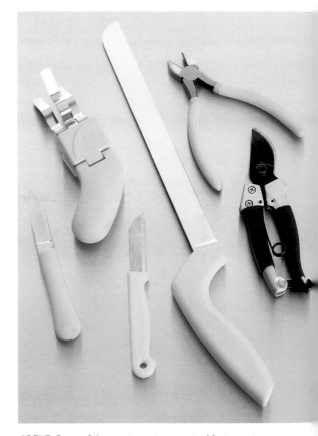

ABOVE Floral foam was invented by Vernon Smithers in the United States and one of the best known brands is 'oasis', from which it takes its common name. It can be purchased in many different forms, sizes and recently in different colours. The green foam is for fresh stems and the brown, which is slightly denser, is intended for use with artificial and dried flowers. Apart from the standard block, there are jumbo blocks, cones, spheres and many frames for the sympathy trade.

LEFT Some useful floral sundries: a roll of bindwire; a roll of floral tape; a roll of floral tac; a roll of double-sided tape; a hank of raffia and of seagrass; a selection of wires; some pearl-headed pins; a roll of gutta-percha tape.

ABOVE Some of the most essential tools to my designs that I keep in my workbox are a choice of good knives to strip, clean and condition the flowers. While I admit that a knife gives you a better cut, personally I prefer to use a strong pair of floristry scissors. A strong pair of spring-loaded secateurs are also very useful when dealing with different strengths of foliage and tough flower stems.

flower care

nomenclature of flowers

The floral designer quickly needs to learn the names of the plants that are available for his or her art. From my own experience I found that looking for their individual costs on invoices so that I could price plant materials quickly speeded up my knowledge of the flower and plant world and I was focused on learning the myriad of flowers and foliage available.

Most plants have popular names that vary with the country and very often from region to region. Generally, however, we use the botanical names, which allows us to exchange information internationally in the world flower market. Latin or Greek is used to describe the plant world and our current system of nomenclature was devised by Karl Linnaeus, a Swedish botanist who lived in the 18th century.

This binomial system consists of two words. The first refers to the genus, which is a group of closely related plants to which the plant belongs and the second is the specific species name. Often a certain hybrid may have more than one species, and each cultivar will have a cultivated variety which is given single quotation marks. For example, beautiful scented sweet peas are called *Lathyrus odoratus* and then each specific variety will have a specific epithet, so that one variety of lilac sweet peas will be called *Lathyrus odoratus* 'Lilac Ripple' where a burgundy and white bicolour will be *Lathyrus odoratus* 'Wiltshire Ripple'.

The international cut flower trade is lucrative and each year large sums are invested in increasing the assortment. This means there is a constant search for new cultivars and cross-breeding hybrids to produce new cultivars. Scientific research also plays a crucial role in improving the vase life of flowers and increasing the strength of flowers so that they travel further. Since floral design has now become so immersed with interior design and the fashion world there has been much more emphasis on trying to predict new trends so that the growers can be one step ahead of demand. The result is that each year the flower assortment becomes larger and the cut flower is a product very much in motion. Varieties come and go, new flowers and foliage become the rage while those with a poor vase life or who lose their popularity disappear from the scene. Sometimes they are flowers that are loved and enjoyed by customers, but because of their unreliability as plants – either they are prone to disease or have an unpredictable yield – they are therefore not profitable enough for the growers.

Every time a new variety is developed the cultivar names fall under the International Code for the Nomenclature for Cultivated Plants. This is the committee which determines the names of plants and sometimes when they are in dispute they determine new names. For example the official generic name of the arum lily is is now *Zantedeschia*. The former name was Calla, and that is often still used. For several years the florist's chrysanthemum was reclassified and given the Latin name of *Dendranthema* but more recently it has been restored to its original Latin name of *Chrysanthemum*. This kind of crossover of names is sometimes very confusing and daunting to the new student of floral art but in a very short time you will astound yourself with how many new flower and plant names you have learnt and are confident about.

when to buy

Generally speaking most of the growers are very good and responsible at presenting their product to the market when it is at the right stage of maturity. Sometimes, however, flowers are cut too early and are not ripe enough or strong enough to flower. There are no hard and fast rules about this because the correct stage for harvesting varies enormously from one species and even among cultivars. Unripe flowers often contain fewer sugars and so as a result they absorb water less well and perform disappointedly. From my own experience it is more likely that there will be unripe flowers available at peak times when the demand is high and the flowers have not quite reached maturity or when flowers are in short supply and the demand is high, such as the wintertime. Generally speaking, most flowers are cut when the bud is showing good colour, although some, such as gerberas, are sold when fully out. Also very occasionally flowers may have been cool-stored for too long and the buds fail to open. Lilies are particularly prone to this and this very often happens around peak periods such as Christmas and Valentine's Day when the sheer demand for products puts too much pressure on the suppliers.

vase life

The value of a cut flower is often perceived by the general public by its longevity or 'vase life'. I have often heard delighted consumers raving about a certain variety because it has last nearly three weeks. Personally I find I am emotionally most attracted to the short-lived often scented varieties, but both in my work and also in my home I too am often drawn to the more practical long-lasting varieties. Once cut from the plant, flowers and foliages begin to age and will eventually wilt and die. This is of course a totally natural and irreversible process, although much research is expended into hybridising varieties that last longer and looking for substances that will prolong the life of cut flowers, from feeding them food and anti-bacterial agents to giving them hormones or even Viagra to keep them holding up longer! The immense importance of the flower industry to the Dutch economy has resulted in most of the research into the factors influencing the longevity of and keeping properties of cut flowers being carried out in the Netherlands, and they have the authoritative position in the world.

conditioning

The term 'conditioning' is the name given to the task of preparing the flowers on arrival from the grower or wholesaler for floral design or for sale as cut flowers. You need to re-cut the stems of all flowers and foliages and place them into a clean container. As a general rule, I would recommend taking 1.5 cm off the end of the stem, creating a slanted cut allowing the end of the stem to be exposed to the maximum surface area of water. Also remove any foliage from the stem that will be in water as this will cause bacteria to grow. And the less leaf on the stem the easier it is for the flower to take up water to the all-important flower head. It is also essential to make sure that the container and the water are clean and free from bacteria. Dirty water may be absorbed into the stem of the flower but it will clog up the vessels within the stems and may then obstruct proper absorption of water by the flower and cause the flower to wilt prematurely. Flowers should never go into water that is too cold as lukewarm water provides more oxygen and is better for the longevity of the flower. Alkaline tap water holds more oxygen than slightly acidic rainwater. There are many nutrient-rich flower foods that can be added to the water which help clean and feed the flower. Some of these are available to the end users and some more specific products are only used by the floral trade and the growers. When you receive your flowers it is a good idea to condition them for several hours as many flowers may have had a very long journey between their grower to the end user and they need to revive before being used for floral design. During the initial 'condition' or drink the flowers will take up water rapidly and so generally deep

water is recommended. All flowers start to pollute their own vase water as they age and some varieties such as the narcissus family are worse than others. It is therefore beneficial if you can change the water often and refresh it with new flower food. There has been a long-established myth among flower arrangers, particularly in the United Kingdom, that it helps the flower to take up water more freely if the stem is cut up vertically in two, or if the ends of woody stems such as lilac or *Viburnum opulus* (guelder rose) are bashed with a wooden mallet. There is absolutely NO scientific evidence for this and in fact all trials on longevity in flowers come out heavily against this. Bashing or cutting the flower ends destroys the valuable cell structure in the stem, which causes some rot and bacteria, which in turn obstructs water absorption. So although this has widely been believed to be beneficial for a long time it is in fact a myth, and makes it much harder for the flower to drink up the water and absorb it up the stem to the most important flower head.

temperature

The room temperature is critical to the longevity of the flowers. Most flowers such as tulips and roses will last considerably longer at 10°C than they will at 20°C. Generally speaking high temperatures and direct sunlight will cause a flower to mature quickly and shorten the vase life. Temperatures between 5°C and 10°C increase the life of nearly all flower varieties, however there are one or two exceptions, such as tropical flowers and the Euphorbia family, who prefer temperature over 16°C. If tropical flowers are kept in refrigerated conditions they very quickly turn black and deteriorate.

evaporation

Cut flowers also need an equilibrium between the water they absorb and the evaporation from the plant. Flower shops are very humid places and very often you will notice that a full flower shop has steamed up windows as the natural process continues after the flowers have been cut from their plant source. Generally speaking the growers try to take the flower to market in water so that it can continue to absorb water. However very often they will be removed from water for transportation to their end user. At this point many flowers and plants lose between 10 and 20 per cent of their weight by evaporation, and however well conditioned when they arrive they will never be restored to their former glory. If the flower has withered completely

there is nothing that can be done to revive it. The speedy transportation of flowers is therefore crucial to the success of the industry. Traders limit evaporation by wrapping the flowers tightly into paper and packing them into boxes. Keeping transportation cool and placing the flowers into water as soon as possible also helps.

Evaporation can also be limited by removing as much of the lower leaf from the stem of each flower, particularly with flowers where there is a lot of lower leaf, such as helianthus, celosia, roses and chrysanthemums.

feeding cut flowers

Plants absorb energy from light by means of their chlorophyll, which is their green colouring-matter, and store it in the form of sugar. The energy within the plant is broken down and used to create the growth and the life cycle for each plant. Once the flower or branch has been cut from the plant, the flowers do not have enough energy to breathe further. This energy shortage can be enhanced by feeding the cut flowers with sugars. Many flowers are fed a post-harvest solution to assist them on their onward journey from the grower to the end user. Many of these solutions contain sugars such as glucose to feed the flower and a disinfectant to prevent bacteria growing. This explains why some of the household remedies for keeping flowers such as adding bleach or sugar to the water have accrued some credence.

Flower food helps to maintain the vase life of flowers. They are more likely to retain a better petal colour and the foliage should hold up better. The flowers are able to retain more energy and the buds and flowers are helped to develop to their full potential. The flowers are less sensitive to damage from the ageing hormone ethylene and this increases their longevity. Hormones created by the plant have a great influence on the life process. One of them, the ageing hormone ethylene gas, influences the life of cut flowers unfavourably. This gas is produced by all plants; some of it remains in the plant but some is released into the surrounding air. This ageing hormone is also created by other vegetation, particularly ripening fruits and vegetables, and air pollution also increases the yields of ethylene. The more ethylene in the room the quicker the flower is likely to die. Although I like to use a lot of fruit and vegetables in my designs, I generally restrict their use to event work or for special occasions when the display is not required to last, because they will shorten the life of the flowers.

Paula's top five tips

1 Check the maturity of the flowers that you are purchasing and unwrap them as soon as you can.
2 Cut the end of the stems obliquely using a sharp knife or a pair of scissors. Remove any foliage that will fall under the water line and any that does not enhance the ornamental value of the flower.
3 Clean buckets with a professional bucket cleaner or a household bleach and disinfectant. Then add clean luke-warm tap water with flower food. Be sure to add the correct ratio of flower food to the quantity of water used.
4 Place the flowers in a well-ventilated storage, preferably at around 6°C and keep an eye on the water level, because the flower will drink a third of its water in the first twelve hours that it is placed back in water after its long journey from the grower.
5 Remove any damaged leaves or flowers and make sure you do not store flowers in proximity to any fruit and vegetables. Also avoid exhaust fumes and cigarette smoke, which can be harmful.

One stem of *Dianthus* 'Rosa Monica,' a standard pink carnation.

flower conditioning

longevity of flowers

Not all cut flowers live for the same length of time. Most varieties live at least five days, some between eight and ten and others will last up to three weeks. The success of a flower is often measured by its vase life and there are many factors which determine how long a flower may live. The most common determining factor is the variety. Fragile dainty garden flowers generally do not last as long as florist-bred flowers such as chrysanthemums, carnations and tropical varieties. Scented varieties also generally do not last as long because a lot of their energy is expended in being fragrant. Many of my favourite perfumed flowers fall into this category, such as sweet peas, tuberosa, jasmine, lily-of-the-valley and stock. The second major factor is the length of time it takes for the flower to make the journey from the grower to the end user. If the flower has been post-harvest treated and kept in water it will have suffered less trauma than a flower that has been harvested in South America, sent by air dry packed to Aalseer in The Netherlands for auction and then re-packed and sent onto North America. Such a flower may have had a minimum of four days without water. In Europe the proximity to the large flower auction in The Netherlands and the use of road transportation means that a lot of flowers are able to travel in water. This means that they are less traumatised and quite simply fresher when they arrive and it makes conditioning far easier. In certain parts of the world where air transportation is the norm the conditioning process can seem more like a 'revival' process, as the flowers have been dry packed for a very long time. It may mean that in those areas certain flowers such as delphiniums and sweet peas have to be sourced locally because they are not good travellers, or they will rarely be used in floral design.

guaranteed life

The importance of how long a flower may live will vary according its purpose. For retail, gift or contract flowers the maximum life is of a prime concern, but for special occasions the flower needs to be in its peak condition to look at its best. For sympathy work, weddings and parties the flowers need to be open and showy, making the ordering and storing of flowers a very vital role in any flower business. Many of the new retailers of flowers are happy to guarantee the life of their flowers in the same way as they date stamp their fresh foods. I can testify that many of their claims are greatly exaggerated, as I have trialed many for consumer research, and at the end of the day each of us has a different opinion on when a bunch of flowers is ready for the bin! I believe a reasonable expectation for a gift bouquet or arrangement should be five days. In my own company we honour this with our customers and take care to ensure that they are given the correct conditioning and maintenance advice in order to get the best from their flowers. Just as there are no guarantees on how long any of us will live, the plant world can be very fragile and unpredictable.

flowers from the garden

If you cut your own flowers it is best to do this in the evening or first thing in the morning. The evening is my preference: at the end of the day the maximum reserves of food are stored in the plant. You can cut your plant material and leave it to drink water and flower food overnight – flowers and foliage will be strong and ready for arranging in the morning.

special tips for certain flowers

Anemone Remember that these flowers, which are available throughout the year, except mid-summer, are very thirsty drinkers, so fill up the vase well. Also it is important to consider that they continue to grow in water so bear this in mind when placing them into arrangements or hand-tied bouquets.

Anthurium These flowers, which originate from South America, and other tropical flowers such as heliconias from warmer climates, do not like the cold and their optimum storage temperature is 18°C. They turn black if they are kept in temperatures below 15°C. They are generally packed into plastic and stored in boxes to protect them from the cold and draughts when in transit. They also are very susceptible to the natural salt found on human skin so avoid handling them – this can result in black decolourisation. These are long lasting flowers – some varieties can last over 50 days – so it is less essential to use flower food with these varieties, but it does not do any harm.

Bouvardia This is a very delicate and pretty flower that is most useful for the bridal trade and delicate arrangements. It is extremely sensitive to dehydration and so it is best transported in water. If it is left out of water for a long time it is very hard, if not impossible, to revive this fragile flower. It is a thirsty flower and so requires deep water and the water level to be checked daily. Usually it is packed and sold by the grower with its own bouvarida flower food, which improves vase life. If the weather is cold halve the normal dose to avoid leaf burn. This special bouvardia food will not harm other varieties. The best storage temperature is 8°C to 10°C.

Euphorbia This is a very big family and there are many varieties that are popular within the flower trade. All euphorbias bleed when their stems are cut, exuding a milky latex substance. This is an irritant to skin and can cause inflammation if placed near the eyes. It is therefore essential to make sure that if you handle these flowers you wash your hands thoroughly. You can simply cut the ends of the stems and condition in the normal way, but if you wish to use these flowers in a glass vase you may want to seal the ends. The best way to do this is to plunge them into boiling water for five seconds. While you are doing this try to protect the flower heads from the effects of the steam by wrapping them in paper.

Carnation Buy standard carnations when they are still firm and not too wide open. Spray carnations should show good colour and the most mature flower should be open. Micro-carnations should be bought when the flower is at least half open. Carnations have nodes along their stems and the stems are thicker here. When conditioning or arranging cut the stem between nodes to allow water to penetrate the stem.

Gerbera These brightly coloured daisy flowers are post-harvest treated and then packed into cardboard boxes. They should be conditioned by cutting the end of their stems and then placing them into water while protecting the flower head. Usually this is done by hanging the flowers into a bucket while their heads are kept flat in their travelling cardboard 'rack'. This enables you to maintain a straight stem and also a well-placed head. Some growers protect the petals by placing them in a plastic ruff that sits at the top of the stem. In some countries they are wired at the wholesale market and many florists wire gerberas externally to keep them upright. If they are fresh they should not need wire and I would only wire them if my design required it or if I was planning to use them in bridal work. Try to avoid touching the flower head as this may cause damage, and after the

One weeping stem of *Euphorbia fulgens* 'Red Surprise'.

One hollow stem of *Hippeastrum* 'Mont Blanc' filled with a bamboo cane to support the flower head.

One fleshy stem of *Hyacinthus orientalis* 'Blue Jacket'. The white bulbous part on the stem will help to support the flower head.

One woody stem of *Syringa vulgaris* 'Hugo Koster'.

initial conditioning do not place them in deep water. They have delicate hairy stems which can go limp and mushy if kept in deep water for a long time.

Helianthus These happy flowers are sensitive to dehydration so do not allow them to dry out completely as they are impossible to revive. The flower is prized but the foliage can be quite unattractive so it is a good idea to remove it. Their thick-stemmed flowers are very thirsty so make sure you put them in very deep water when you first condition them. They are very sensitive to bacteria and so benefit greatly from flower food. Make sure that the vase you put them in is scrupulously clean and avoid earthenware vases in which bacteria can multiply in the pores of the earthenware surface.

Hippeastrum These elegant flowers are sold dried packed into boxes. They have cavernous long hollow stems. The best way to condition them is to take off a couple of centimetres from the end of the stem and then insert a bamboo cane into the stem to protect the head while the stem takes water to the flower head. Most amaryllis have four heads and they take over a week to open fully. These flowers have been heavily hybridised and so the head is very large and the cane in the hollow stem helps to protect the stem when the flower is fully extended. This also helps to protect them from 'committing suicide' when placed in water over the edge of a glass vase, and also helps when using them in foam and intricate designs. The ends can split and become slimy so try to re-cut the stems every two or three days or even use some sellotape if visible or florists' tape if not visible around the bottom to protect the end.

Hyacinth This wonderful scented spring bulb is usually cut just above the bulb and it is vital to the strength of the stems to try to keep as much of the base on the stem as possible. Cut the minimum

off the end, trying to keep as much of the woody white stem to help support the stem when all the little fragrant florets have opened fully. Hyacinth bulbs are often cultivated in sandy soils so rinse off any grains before using the flowers.

Iris When you buy iris make sure that they are showing good colour for at least 3 cm because if they are too immature the buds will not open. Iris are short-living flowers and they are very susceptible to bacteria, particularly botrytis, which is a fungus that grows on flowers. It is essential to dispose of these flowers if they are past their best as they can infect other flowers. Although I adore flag iris and grow many varieties in my garden I only tend to use the commercial iris on its own massed together where you can also appreciate its long elegant stem. Its short life and its star shape make it difficult to use with other flower heads.

Lathyrus Sweet peas are sensitive to dehydration and so they are often wrapped with water to keep them moist. Immediately re-cut the stems and place in no more than 5 cm of water. Try not to bunch them too tightly together or crowd them in a bucket, as they are very sensitive to botrytis. They naturally generate heat and can quickly start to wilt if they are massed together.

Lilium Lilies can often be cut too early or cold stored for too long so that they never reach their full potential. Make sure that a few buds are fully developed and that some are showing the colour of the flower. Look carefully at the bud to see that it is not unnaturally withered and also make sure that the foliage is lovely and green before you purchase. Although the anthers look lovely, they pollinate and can ruin the face of the flower as well as stain furniture and clothes so pinch off the anthers from the end of the filament. This does not damage the flower. If any pollen does get onto clothes, try to remove it with adhesive tape and do not wet.

Matthiola This gorgeous scented flower, commonly known as stocks, is another short-lived beauty. Prized for its wonderful scent, like all fragrant flowers it expends a lot of its energy in its scent to the detriment of its life. It is also very sensitive to dehydration and should not be left to dry out. As a member of the Brassica family it can have a pungent smell if the water gets contaminated, so it is essential to use flower food. As it is very sensitive to bacteria make sure the vase is scrupulously clean and avoid earthenware vessels, which have pores in which the bacteria can multiply.

Narcissus Although you can buy daffodils in tight bud showing no colour it is essential to purchase the multiple headed Narcissus such as 'Paperwhite', 'Ziva' or 'Churchill' when they are fully developed and loose. If they are cut too immature they do not form fully and can be very disappointing. All narcissus produce slime that can be damaging to other flowers. It is essential to condition them for at least 24 hours before mixing them with other flowers and it is best to use narcissus flower food that has been specially developed to neutralise the effects of the slime.

Nerine Nerines should also be showing colour and at least one bud should be loose when you purchase them. These elegant flowers do not like temperature below 2°C and are generally very long lasting flowers that are grown for the trade all through the year, but are in greater supply for the last five months of the year.

Orchid There are a huge variety of orchids, which generally require no special conditioning and are extremely long lasting. They are usually packed in water phials to keep them happy during transit so on arrival re-cut the stems and place in water with flower food.

They are sensitive to temperature below 15°C and really hate draughts. The more delicate phalenopsis orchid can be refreshed by submerging in lukewarm water if they have become flaccid.

Papaver Sadly most poppies are short lived, both in their natural habitat and also as cut flowers. *Papaver nudicaule* last between six and nine days. Most poppies are supplied with their stems singed because they exude a milky sap. If you need to trim the stems, it is essential that you re-singe them with a naked flame. Oriental and somniferum varieties generally last about four days, but they are useful to a florist for their seed head, which can be used green or dried in long-lasting arrangements or Christmas decorations. The seed head is tremendously long lasting.

Paeonia Peonies are gorgeous seasonal flowers, which are susceptible to bacteria and benefit enormously from flower food. To help open tight buds, spray occasionally with water, which helps to dissolve the sugars that can prevent the buds from opening fully. They are very sensitive to temperature fluctuations so keep them in a cool spot.

Rosa Roses should be purchased when the bud is fully developed and showing colour with fresh leaves. Flower food is essential. Re-cut stems frequently and refresh often for maximum life. Remove thorns and lower foliage with a sharp knife without damaging the stem.

Tulip Tulips should be purchased when the bud is fully developed and showing colour. The foliage should show no disease. If the tulips are droopy, which happens to the more heavily hybridised varieties, such as parrot or double tulips, re-cut, wrap them in paper and place in a cold spot for several hours so they can straighten up. Tulips continue to grow in a vase and it is important to remember this if mixing them with other flowers.

One hairy singed stem of *Papaver nudicaule*.

One woody stem of Rosa 'Coolwater'.

hand-tied flowers

A hand tied bouquet is simply a bunch of flowers and foliage that has been spiralled in the hand and then tied at the binding point ready to be placed into a vase. It can often be aqua packed (wrapped with water) so that it makes the perfect gift. It takes most people a few attempts to get the hang of this, but after five or six attempts it soon becomes quite instinctual! It is certainly the design I use the most and is one of the most versatile arrangements. Mastering the skill of the hand-tied is central to creating many of my trademark designs. When I started my business nearly twenty years ago, the hand-tied bouquet was very popular in continental Europe but scarcely seen in the United Kingdom. In the last 15 years it has become very popular here and is now gaining popularity all around the world. It is most regularly used as a gift item to take to someone's home or to have delivered by a florist. However, its uses have now become so widespread that everyone who loves to arrange flowers wants to learn this skill to enable them to create contemporary vase arrangements for their own home. Looser, flat backed versions can be used as swags or chair backs for Christmas displays or weddings and sleek small versions can be used as bridal bouquets or bridesmaids' posies. Tightly packed bouquets can be used to top vases for a more formal look in corporate or event work.

When you are selecting the materials for a hand-tied arrangement I recommend that you start with a bunch of straight and strong flowers such as a bunch of roses. You need at least 20 stems to make a bunch and 25 to 35 is the average. Thoroughly clean the lower stems to make them free of thorns and foliage. It is impossible if there is greenery at the binding point, as the bunch becomes difficult to handle and it is then hard to achieve a good spiral. In any case, you need to keep the stems nice and clean so that when you put the flowers back in water there is no greenery in the vase to prematurely age the bouquet.

An early summer hand-tied bouquet mixes the spring flowers of lilac, guelder roses, anemone, and ranunculus with summer peonies.

simple hand-tied bouquet

This simple hand-tied bouquet of vibrantly coloured roses is the best way to practise your hand-tying technique. The flowers are straight and sturdy and they are one of the easiest to use. A mass of the same flower is easier than a mix of different flowers and foliages. I like to edge this design with folded aspidistra leaves, which are inexpensive and make for a very fetching contemporary bouquet. One round of leaves is very effective, but you can continue to several rounds to accentuate the massed roses within.

materials

20 *Rosa* 'Ruby Red'
20 *Rosa* 'Coolwater'
20 *Rosa* 'Milano'
15 stems of aspidistra leaves
a roll of cellotwist
a roll of ribbon

step by step

1 First, strip all the foliage from the stems; working from the top to the bottom of the stem, prise off the leaves and thorns with a sharp knife.

2 Taking the central rose in your left hand (if you are right-handed, vice versa if you are left handed), place the next rose to the left of the first at an angle of around 25 degrees. Place the third one just left of that until you have a fan of 7 stems. At this point, start to turn them by taking your other hand and twisting them about a half turn. Next add another five stems in exactly the same manner and then twist again.

3 Keep adding roses in this pattern until you have a nice round dome of roses. Tie tightly with the floral cellotwist at the binding point where you have been holding the roses.

4 Loop the aspidistra leaf by placing a small piece of pot tape around the stem. The leaf will last well like this as the stem is still in water. Edge the bouquet with the folded aspidistra leaves. Finally make a 3-loop ribbon bow and tie it around the stems.

grouped bouquet

Putting flowers in groups allows you to use more striking colour combinations than when you mix them all up. It allows you to experiment with both colours and also the textural element of the plant material. Grouping flowers is currently very fashionable and makes any design look more contemporary.

materials

5 stems of *Rosa* 'Sphinx'
5 stems of *Viburnum opulus* 'Roseum'
5 stems of *Hyacinthus orientalis* 'Blue Star'
10 stems of *Anemone coronaria* 'Mona Lisa Blue'
3 stems of *Rosa* 'Wow'
3 stems of *Rosa* 'Sunbeam'
3 stems of *Hydrangea* 'Challenge Blue'
a *Chrysanthemum* 'Shamrock'
a bunch of *Narcissus grootkronige* 'Cheerfulness'
3 stems of *Rosa* 'Grand Prix'
a bunch of *Ranunculus* 'Ranobelle Inra'
a bunch of coral fern (*Gleichenia polypodiodes*)
a bunch of *Hedera helix*
5 stems of *Hypericum inodorum* 'King Flair'

step by step

1 Taking a central group of 3 'Sphinx' roses start to build up your grouped hand-tie by placing plant material at a 30-degree angle to the left of the previous placement. Every three or so placements twist the bouquet in your hand so that you are working on all sides and creating a spiral posy. Add bunches of foliage throughout to create a more textural effect

2 Continue building up the tied bunch so that you have a good mix of colour throughout, and as you continue the plant placements will be at a 45-degree angle to create a nice rounded shape. Edge with the coral fern and tie at the binding point where you have been holding the flowers with floral bind wire. Trim the ends of the bouquet so that the flowers fit neatly into the vase and top up with water and flower food.

tropical bouquet

This hand-tied bouquet is often also known as a limited design or a line bouquet. The principle of adding the flowers is the same as with a hand-tied round bouquet except that you are keeping the back flatter and the final design will be essentially front facing or it will have one more attractive side. I use this design when more architectural flowers are chosen and very often when the customer requires a more masculine bouquet. In this design there are two distinct areas of interest: the striking shape of the heliconias with the willow; and the denser lower area filled with textural flowers and foliage.

materials

5 *Heliconia stricta* 'Huber'
5 *Leucospermum cordiolium* ' Sunrise'
1 thick stem of date palm (*Phoenix roebelenii*)
5 *Monstera Ideliciosa* leaves
5 branches of contorted willow (*Salix matsudana tortuosa*)
5 stems of *Bixa orellana*
Cordyline fructicosa 'Negri' leaves
a length of raffia
a roll of Japanese paper

step by step

1 First remove all the lower foliage from the flowers and lay them out in bunches ready arranged. Take one piece of willow and place one heliconia slightly to the left of the willow at an angle of 25 degrees.

2 Add the rest of the willow and the tall heliconias at the same angles to the left and right of the central flowers. Next arrange a group of the leucospermums to the left of the bouquet.

3 Add the rest of the plant material in groups allowing the date palm the central position so that it can

trail over the front, Edge the bouquet with monstera leaves and then tie with raffia.

4 Fold a length of Japanese paper and place around the binding point. Create a bow from several lengths of raffia by making two loops and then tie through the centre to create a figure of eight. Add to the binding point to secure the paper.

bouquet in a vase

The overwhelming majority of my designs are made in glass vases because they allow you to create a very sculptural design by placing different plant material or media in the vase. This particular design was inspired by the discovery of a new treatment for roses where this large 'Avalanche' rose has been dipped in a special solution of paint to create a flocked effect which ironically makes a natural rose look almost like a fabric flower.

materials

1 large clear glass urn with a frosted plinth
1 frosted vase
a length of floral bind wire
a pair of scissors
1 kilo of marshmallows
a bunch of *Viburnum tinus*
a bunch of *Camellia japonica*
a bunch of *Ranunculus* 'Cappucino Pink'
10 stems of *Rosa* 'Marshmallow'
10 stems of *Tulipa* 'First Class'
12 stems of *Rosa* 'Barbie'

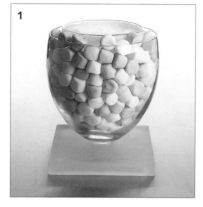

step by step

1 Fill the bottom of the urn with marshmallows. Place the frosted glass vase into the centre of it and then stuff the sides with marshmallows.

2 Taking a central 'Marshmallow' rose and a piece of foliage start placing plant material to the left of the central rose at an angle of about 25 degrees.

3 Add a sprig of *Viburnum tinus*, a ranunculus, a 'Barbie' rose and a tulip, all slightly to the left of the piece before. At this point you need to turn it in your hand so take your right hand and twist it.

4 Place the flowers and foliage at the same angle. Continue adding and twisting every five or six pieces of plant material The stems should start to fan out and you can start to see the spiralled stem of the posy.

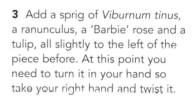

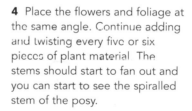

5 Continue until you have used all the plant material. As the bunch starts to grow the flowers and foliage will be placed at more of a 45 degree angle. Using the floral bind wire bind and tie tightly where you have been holding the bunch. Trim all the stems with a diagonal cut; if the bouquet is well balanced, it will stand on its own stems.

6 Fill the central vase with water and place the bouquet in the centre of the vase. Gently recut the binding point so that the flowers loosen up a little bit and just fall over the edge of the vase.

wrapped bouquet

Round bouquets can be wrapped in a number of ways. The most common wrapping is cellophane, which can also be used to aqua pack the flowers so they are delivered in water. The wrapping helps to protect the flowers as well as making them more decorative. We also use tissue and Japanese papers, as well as fabric and deconet to enhance our gift bouquets. Filleted banana leaves make a lovely natural biodegradable foil for floral bouquets and are a favourite of ours for rose bouquets for Valentine's Day.

materials

10 stems of *Tulipa* 'Winterberg'
10 stems of cream *Ranunculus asiaticus*
5 stems of cream *Hyacinthus orientalis* 'City of Haalem'
7 stems of *Rosa* 'Alexis'
5 stems of *Viburnum opulus* 'Roseum'
5 stems of *Skimmia japonica* 'Fructo Alba'
3 stems of berried *Hedera helix*
a roll of oasis bindwire
a roll of cream deconet
a roll of cellophane
a length of ribbon

step by step

1 Carefully remove any foliage from the lower stems of all the flowers. Arrange your materials in groups and begin to make the spiral bouquet by taking one central flower and placing plant material slightly at an angle to the left of the first central flower. This may start at an angle of around 30 degrees and as you get to the end of the bouquet may be more like 45 degrees. Continue doing this with the three other stems and then twist the bunch round in your hand and then add another five stems to the left. Continue twisting the bouquet every five pieces of plant material so you are working on all sides. Remember to continue to use pieces of foliage throughout the bouquet to help create the structure and add interest to the bouquet.

2 When you have added all the plant material, tie with the oasis bind wire at the point where you have been holding the bouquet. Cut a piece of thick cellophane and place it around the base of the stems to create a bag for water. Tie the cellophane securely and fill the bag with water.

3 Cut a length of net to go around the bouquet and tie around the middle with a 3-looped bow.

LEFT Try this selection for an alternative bouquet:
7 stems of *Gloriosa rothschildiana*
10 stems of *Rosa* 'Milano'
10 stems of *Rosa* 'Supergreen'
7 yellow *Zantedeschia aethiopia* 'Florex Gold'
10 stems of *Hypericum* 'Brown Flair'
7 stems of *Chrysanthemum* 'Shamrock'
half a bunch of bear grass (*Xerophyllum tenax*)
10 stems of hard *Ruscus hypophyllum*

wedding posy

For over a decade the round hand-tied posy has been the most popular design for wedding celebrations. Generally we do not cover the stems as many brides prefer the natural 'just picked' look and rarely do we cover the stems of the attendant's posies. When requested to cover the stems with ribbon or fabric we often use double-sided tape.

materials

7 stems of 'Sarah Bernhardt' peonies
10 stems of pink *Astilbe* 'Erika'
10 stems of *Alchemilla mollis*
10 stems of pale pink sweet peas
10 stems of bicolour pink *Rosa* 'Carnival'
a length of bind wire
a roll of oasis pot tape
a roll of double-sided 'carpet' tape
a roll of matching ribbon
a pair of floristry scissors
a pair of ribbon scissors

CLOCKWISE FROM TOP RIGHT The finished step-by-step wedding posy; a bridal bouquet of white 'Akito' roses hand-tied with *Bouvardia* 'Diamond White;' a posy of 'Vendella' roses, Pink rancunulus, blue muscari and *Bouvardia* Diamond Pink, and two bridesmaids' posies of pink ranunculus edged with galax leaves.

step by step

1 Strip all the lower foliage off the ends of the stems and clean the thorns off the roses by using the edge of a sharp knife. When they are ready place each variety in piles so that you can mix up the varieties as you begin to spiral your posy. Start with a central rose, then add a stem of *Alchemilla mollis* at a 25-degree angle and then a stem of Astillbe to the left of that at the same angle and a sweet pea in the same way. After that you will need to start to twist it in your hand so you are working on all sides of the design.

2 Continue adding five or so stems and then twisting the bouquet until you have achieved a lovely spiral-stemmed bouquet. Tie with bindwire at the point you have been holding the bouquet, which is known as the binding point. Bindwire is a floral product created

especially to tie spiralled boquets firmly It has a central wire covered by paper so that it gives a tight tie without damaging any of the more delicate stems.

3 Starting at the binding point, tape together the spiralled stems with floral foam tape, working down to the bottom of the handle.

4 Next add two strips of double-sided tape down either side of the taped handle. Take a roll of ribbon and, starting from the top, bind around the handle by diagonal loops until you reach the bottom and then bind all the way up to the top again.

5 Cut off the additional ribbon at the binding point of the bouquet and then make a bow from three loops of ribbon with one central tie. Fasten the ribbon to the binding point with the bow.

victorian posy

Flowers of concentric circles are often known as Victorian posies, and are sometimes referred toin North America as 'Biedermeier designs'. The word 'Biedermeier' actually refers to a period of furniture design, painting and literature in Germany and Austria during the period from 1815 to 1848. Concentric circle arrangements were also the height of fashion at that time in Victorian England. These tightly packed rings of the same type of flowers are sometimes wired, but more often are hand tied. This delightful posy is a modern take on an old idea with its structural ring of fresh spring contorted willow.

materials

20 stems of *Tulipa* 'Winterberg'
1 *Rosa* 'Alexis'
25 stems of *Narcissus tazetta* 'Avalanche'
5 stems of *Salix babylonica* 'Tortuosa'
50 stems of *Muscari botryoides* 'Album'
50 stems of *Fritillaria meleagris*

step by step

1 Choose a good specimen of 'Alexis' rose for the centre of the bouquet and then place bunches of 5 stems of white muscari all the way round the rose. Tie at the binding point to secure the flowers.

2 Working slightly further down from the muscari add a ring of the narcissi to be the same width as the muscari. Secure again with oasis bindwire.

3 Add a row of tulips. Secure these again with oasis bindwire. This massing of heads where it overlaps is sometimes referred to as a pave (see page 60).

4 Twist the five stems of contorted willow into a small wreath that will fit snugly around the posy. Tape with floral tape two heavy wires and secure them into either side of the ring.

5 Complete the posy by adding bunches of the fritillaria around the posy. Place the wreath ring around the base of the flower heads and secure by placing the two taped wires through the centre of the posy. Finally trim the ends of the posy and add a 3-looped bow.

This ballerina bouquet includes *Matthiola incana* 'Francesca,' *Zantedeschia vivalda*, variegated *Hedera helix*, *Lupinus* 'Little Eugenie,' astilbe japonica europa, solomon's seal, *Syringa vulgaris* 'Dark Kosta' and *Rosa* 'Prima Donna.'

ballerina bouquet

This over-arm bouquet is designed for presentations on stage. It is a formal style of arm bouquet where the flowers are arranged as a teardrop with an extension of the stems showing for the recipient to hold. Usually carried in the fold of the arm, this style of bouquet can be used for weddings where it is known as an over-arm bouquet but is more often requested for the stage in Europe. In North America where it is called a presentation bouquet it is also often used for beauty pageants. In London I arrange them for divas of the opera or much more commonly for ballerinas performing at the Royal Opera House or The Coliseum.

materials

5 stems of *Gloriosa rothschildiana*
10 stems of *Lupinus* 'Terracotta'
10 stems of *Matthiola incana* 'Francesca'
10 stems of *Viburnum opulus* 'Roseum'
7 stems of double lilac *Eustoma russellianum* 'Mariachi Misty Blue'
10 stems of *Panicum* 'Fountain'
10 stems of Solomon's seal (*Polygonatum multiflorum*)
10 stems of *Amaranthus cordatus*
a roll of floral bind wire
a pair of scissors
a roll of organza ribbon

step by step

1 Clean all the lower foliage from the stems of the flowers and plants. Using a knife, prise off the thorns from the roses to reveal straight and clean stems. Taking some of the trailing foliage begin the bouquet using the solomon's seal, amaranthus and *Viburnum opulus*.

2 Continue to build up the bouquet, adding the flowers as you go along, taking each variety and placing it in a zigzag across the centre of the design.

3 You are aiming to make a diamond shaped outline with a profile that is triangular with the highest point in the centre of the bouquet and tailing down to the binding point. Add any of the fillers such as the fountain grass into any of the gaps you have and then tie with the floral bind wire.

4 Trim with a bow by making three loops of ribbon and tying another length through the centre.

materials

1 small plastic water phial
1 laurel leaf
a length of raffia
3 stems of *Hedera helix*
a branch of *Viburnum tinus*
5 heads of *Helleborus orientalis*

napkin rings

Floral napkin ties can be a lavish touch to a large
formal celebration or a rather personal simple touch
for a dinner party. For formal events we often do a
ribboned bow and a flower for each guest or on
some occasions just for the female guests. Little
posies placed on each napkin can be a more
personal way of decorating the table than creating
single or even several centrepieces.

step by step

1 First wash the ivy and leave to
dry. Place two stems of trailing ivy
around a napkin twisting over itself
so that it stays in place.

2 Fill the phial with water and cover
with a laurel leaf tied with raffia.
Arrange your flower heads
into a little diamond-shaped posy.
Cut the ends of the stems neatly
and place into the phial. Tuck the
water phial into the twisted stems
of trailing ivy.

chair backs

A floral chair back has become very popular for weddings and can be used for both formal and informal occasions. Most often a chair back is a tied sheaf of flowers. One of the reasons for the growth in popularity is the huge diversity of venues that are now licensed to hold weddings. A row of chair backs enhances an aisle for a ceremony or marks out the top table in situations where the bride and groom have chosen to have a round table instead of the more formal long one-sided top table. Very often we move them from the ceremony to the reception so they get to be used throughout the wedding day. They are usually attached to the side for an aisle and centrally placed on the chair for a top table. The choice of flowers can make them look formal or informal. The use of one type of flower such as the hydrangea creates a more contemporary look.

materials

5 stems of *Gloriosa Rothschildiana*
5 *Helianthus annus* 'Sunrich Orange'
5 *Rosa* 'Milano'
3 *Viburnum opulus* 'Roseum'
3 stems of yellow *genista*
½ bunch of berried *hedera*
7 stems of *Asparagus umbellatus*
1 bunch of *Skimmia japonica*
'Rubella'
5 stems of *camellia*
a pair of scissors
a roll of oasis bind wire

step by step

1 Find one piece of flat foliage to use as the base for this hand-tied. Build up the foliage to create a triangle using some flat foliage and some trailing foliage.

2 Continue adding bushy foliage such as the skimmia and ivy berries to improve the profile of the chair back. The highest point of the foliage should be above the point where you are holding it.

3 Begin to arrange your flowers by loosening your hand and threading your flowers through the foliage and into the desired place. Start at the end and working on alternate sides place each variety of flowers through the design to the base. Finally place the roses and sunflowers across the design and add some extra foliage at the binding point to trail over the front. Tie with oasis bind wire.

4 Attach to the chair with ribbon.

OPPOSITE TOP LEFT
One perfect stem of white *Hydrangea macrophylla* 'Schneeball' make a modern decoration for this classic chair.

OPPOSITE TOP RIGHT
Trailing ivy and berried ivy have been wired to create a garland across the top of the chair which has then had *Eustoma russellianum* 'Echo Pure White', cream *Rosa* 'Gracia' spray rose, *Lathyrus odoratus*, *Rosmarinus officinalis* and ranunculus wired into it.

OPPOSITE BOTTOM LEFT
A hand-tied bunch of margarite daisies (*Argyranthemum frutescens*) with a natural raffia bow.

OPPOSITE BOTTOM RIGHT
A floral lei of white Singaporian dendrobium orchids have been strung together on a heavy transparent thread.

arrangements

Strictly speaking an arrangement is defined as plant material in a container. This actually would include many of my hand-tied bouquets, because once they are placed into a container they become an arrangement. However, in our flower school here in London we first teach students the art of hand tying and then move onto arranging. For an arrangement, the starting point is usually the container. Arrangements come in many forms and can be small or large vase arrangements with no mechanics. They can also be huge urns and trailing mantelpieces with sturdy mechanics to keep the flowers in place and the arrangement well balanced. By far the most commonly used mechanics for arranging flowers is the green foam sometimes known by its brand name 'oasis'. For larger arrangements or for delicate flowers such as muscari or heavy stemmed flowers, such as hyacinths, chicken wire is preferable because it allows the flowers to drink more freely. Grids of tape, wires, pin holders, gel and even cellophane and moss are all examples of the mechanics used to anchor and support flowers, as well as natural products such as twigs, shells and stones.

The style and shape of an arrangement is determined by its destination and purpose. A table arrangement may be low and small enough to fit the table and allow the seated guests to see and talk to one another, or it may be so vast and impressive that it has one or two tiers so the guests sit under the design. For corporate arrangements and weekly contract work, one of the main concerns is that the flowers last well, and so here the emphasis is on choosing reliable plants that all look good together and last around the same amount of time.

Tall glass vase filled with jalapeno peppers and topped with contorted willow with *Physallis alkekengi* 'Jumbo' and orange *Euphorbia fulgens* 'Sunstream'.

securing flowers

Green foam is more commonly known by its major brand 'oasis'. The accidental discovery in North America of this compound which absorbs water and is principally is used to hold the flowers in place, and provide them with a source of vital water for their longevity, radically changed the way flowers could be arranged and particularly delivered. It is largely responsible for the creation of less naturalistic trends in floristry from the 1960s onwards when it became more commonly used.

floral foam spheres

materials

30–35 mixed mini gerberas in monochromatic colours
a teardrop-shaped vase approx. 22cm high
a 10-cm green floral foam sphere

Spherical foam balls are available in a number of sizes and are useful for creating pomanders, topiary or massed round designs. Balls can either be impaled on a stick or vase to create a standard topiary form or they can be hung. Small hanging decorations are usually suspended from a ribbon and are often created for bridesmaids. Large spherical arrangements are created by wiring together two hanging baskets filled with floral foam and covered with 2.5cm chicken wire. A decoration of this size is often used to hang in large halls or marquees.

step by step

1 Soak the floral foam until the air bubbles cease to rise. Press it hard down onto the ridge of the vase so that it is firmly balanced.

2 Starting from the base work up to the top to cover one half of the ball with the mini gerberas (which are sometimes known as germini) heads. Trim the stems to about 2cm long to avoid breaking up the floral foam too much.

3 Continue with the other half of the ball until there is no longer any floral foam visible.

floral foam ring

Round floral foam rings are made in a multitude of widths. The large 35-cm and 40-cm wreath frames are very useful for large table centres for round 1.5m or 2m banqueting tables. Into the centre you can place bowls or storm lanterns filled with candles. Often we might group flowers together to create a very colourful table centre or here we have used the flowers in a very natural way, grouping some flowers but using the length of others to give the arrangement movement and rhythm.

materials

5 stems of sunflower (*Helianthus annus* 'Orit')
1 bunch of green *Rancunculus* 'Clooney'
10 stems of *Rudbeckia hirta*
a bunch of white flowering *Skimmia confusa* 'Kew Green'
a bunch of *Genista tinctoria* 'Royal Gold"
7 stems of *Zantedeschia aethiopica* 'Best Gold'
a bunch of chanel *mimosa acacia crassa*
3 bunches of *Galax erceolata*
a bunch of flexigrass (*Xanthorrhoea australis*)
a bunch of pussy willow (*Salix caprea*)
7 *Anthurium crystallinum* leaves
a 16-cm round wreath frame
9 floating candles
a straight-sided glass bowl

step by step

1 Soak the floral ring until the bubbles cease to rise. Trim the top of the corners of the oasis to make it easier to put the plant material in. Edge round the ring with galax leaves taking care to cover the plastic base.

2 Place groups of foliage at different heights and depths along the ring, starting with the skimmia, then the flowering genista, and then create loops encircling the ring using stems of the flexigrass.

3 Place stems of pussy willow into the oasis by putting the stem end in and then the other end in so that they are orbiting the ring. Place the 7 anthurium leaves into the oasis so that they are all pointing the same anti-clockwise way. Then place groups of rudbeckia, ranunculus and sunflowers into the ring.

4 To complete the rhythm of the ring place the ends of the stems of the calla lilies into the foam and then twist them under the willow so that they follow the anti-clockwise movement of the design. Finally, add sprigs of the mimosa around the ring, filling any gaps.

5 Place a glass bowl into the centre of the ring. Fill with water and floating candles.

using coloured floral foam

There are two main types of floral foam; green which is absorbent for fresh flowers and brown which is denser and created for dried or artificial flowers. Recently a number of different colours of floral foam have been created and this is semi absorbent and can be used for fresh flowers or dried or artificial flowers. I use coloured floral foam when creating fruit bowls.

materials

I block of orange floral foam
5 oranges
9 stems of *Rosa* 'Milva'
9 stems of *Rosa* 'Wow'
30 stems of *Rosa* 'Milano'
10 stems of *Germini* 'Aisha' (mini gerbera)
7 stems of *Leucospurmum cordifolum* 'Tango'
a bunch of *Calendula officianalis*
'Greenheart Orange'
15 stems of *Gloriosa rothschildiana*
8 stems of *Celosia cristata* 'Bombay Pink'
7 stems of *Viburnum opulus* 'Roseum'
a bunch of *Camellia japonica*
a bunch of ivy berries (*Hedera helix*)
20 stems of *Ruscus hypophyllum*
a tall-stemmed lead glass fruit bowl

step by step

1 Soak the floral foam in water and then place upright in the centre of the container. Meanwhile cut slices of orange just under 1cm thick, and place around the edge of the bowl. Using a thin strip of floral foam tape the foam securely into the bowl. Trim off the corner of the floral foam to make it easier to put the plant material in at all angles.

2 Taking the three types of foliage establish the outline of your arrangement and completely cover the floral foam before adding any flowers. The coloured floral foam requires slightly more and denser foliage than green foam.

3 Next add the thick stemmed flowers such as celosia and the woody stemmed flowers such as the *Leucospurmum* and *Viburnum opulus*. Next add the roses in groups and then the marigolds and mini germini.

4 Finally add the delicate flowerheads of the *Gloriosa rothschildiana* and top up the water in the bowl together with added flower food.

fixing with tape

materials

16–20 bunches of *muscari*
175 bunches of flexigrass
(*Xanthorrhoea australis*)
a roll of tape
(thin green floral foam tape
is best but thin clear sticky
tape will work just as well)

Grids of tape like this are very useful for shallow glass containers where green floral foam would be inappropriate or difficult to use. I usually use grids for low glass bowls, particularly crystal glass. Here I also chose to use a grid of tape rather than floral form because the massed stems of muscari would have been almost impossible to pack so densely into foam and they will survive better with more access to water. The tape holds the bunches of flowers in place while allowing them to drink the water freely.

step by step

1 Line the glass dish with swirls of flexigrass so that it fits snugly around the edge. Using single lengths of floral foam or clear tape make lines of one way and then across the other to create a grid of tape with holes of around 2 cm square.

2 Fill with water mixed with flower food, which will keep the water clean and free from bacteria. This is very important when you are using plant material such as the flexigrass below the water line, Working from one side of the bowl place small bunches of muscari into each square until you have covered the whole grid.

using a pinholder

materials

20 *Allium* 'Purple Sensation'
a glass dish
a 6-cm flower pin holder
a roll of 'Floraltac' adhesive

for the base

40 stems of *Tulipa* 'Blue Diamond'
18 stems of *Hyacinthus orientalis*
'Minos'
24 stems of *Rosa* 'Blue Pacific'
12 stems of *Viburnum opulus*
'Roseum'
24 stems of *Rosa* 'Green Planet'
40 baby aubergines
40 stems of *Skimmia laureola*
12 branches of *Senecio greyii*
a bunch of coral fern (*Gleichenia
polypodiodes*)
10 stems of *Ruscus hypophyllum*
a 45-cm floral foam wreath frame

Pinholders are very useful for anchoring a few flowers into a low container. They are used mostly for minimal flower designs or for Japanese Ikebana. I tend to use them for tall architectural flowers such as members of the allium, iris, strelitzia, helleconia and agapanthus families.

step by step

1 'Floraltac' is a waterproof clay which has been designed especially for the floral industry to secure and anchor objects into an arrangement. Take an inch of the 'floral tac' clay and rub it together in your hands to make it warm. This makes it more adhesive. Place it in the centre of the dish and push the pinholder down on the adhesive clay until it is firm.

2 Cut the ends of the alliums and impale them on the pinholder, ensuring that they are all the same height. Start in the centre of the pinholder and work to the outside until the pin holder is completely covered.

3 Soak the wreath frame in a large bucket until the air bubbles cease to rise. This should take about five minutes. Take care not to force the foam under water because this can create an air lock in the foam and then it does not retain the water. Cut the outside and the inside edge off the floral foam ring so you can now line the edge of the frame with coral fern. Continue to cover the foam with groups of foliage. I have used grey senecio, white flowering skimmia and dark green ruscus. Next, add the flowers in groups of odd numbers. Wire up the aubergines by placing a heavy stub wire through the base and twisting the two legs together and then placing them into the ring in large clumps.

containers

One of the aspects that made my work original was to use containers that were not intended for flower arranging, such as fruit bowls, plates and dishes. This has now become such a trend that many companies specialise in making items just for the flower trade. Currently huge glass vases that contain the flower arrangement within are in vogue. Cube containers, minimal containers with an Eastern influence and vessels made of zinc and metal also proved very popular. New trends emerge as changes in fashion and interior design come and go!

Wire baskets that can be filled with moss are one of my favourites for natural summer flowers. Here an urn and a basket shape have been filled with ivy, hypericum, senecio, skimmia, veronica, hebe, hydrangea, sweet pea and 'Sterling silver' roses.

LEFT Two stems of vanda orchid have been arranged in a zinc moon vase with 3 stems of anthurium leaves, 5 stems of trailing weeping willow and a handful of spanish moss.

BELOW As I am very attracted to brightly coloured flowers I am also interested in finding containers to accentuate this or to be very feminine. I sometimes cover vases in fabric or use little bags such as this beaded bag to contain the flowers. This simple arrangement is a more contemporary twist on the traditional basket arrangement. Ten stems of the pale pink rose Universe have been hand tied and aqua packed and placed into a small sequinned basket for a very feminine arrangement.

Rustic containers such as terracotta pots or oil jars from Provençe fashioned out of the earth always look good with flowers because they are natural and in empathy with the bouquet. They may not currently be as fashionable as they were but for me they are still items I return to each year. I also like wooden trugs and wire baskets for the same reason – they are classical and pleasing. If you are choosing a container for a few flowers, such as the beautiful vanda orchids pictured above, you need a strong vase design. A few flowers need a strong form and this is why if you study oriental floristry such as Ikebana the container is such an intergral part of the design. The colour and shape of the container are also vital considerations and they should be in sympathy with the flower colour and a suitable size for your chosen plant material.

Another important consideration when chosing a container is that it is sturdy enough to hold the mechanics and the flowers. Large arrangements which may use urns and

pedestals need to be heavy or well weighted because the water and plant material needed will be very heavy and can easily be top heavy if the base is not substantial. We use a lot of fibreglass urns and plinths for our weddings and also laquerware, taking care to make sure the arrangements are well balanced in the containers. For heavy fruit arrangements you need to use heavy metal bases because the weight of the moss and fruit will be too substantial for weaker containers.

I personally prefer to customise my own container and make it part of the overall design. The arrangement then takes on a much

LEFT A heavy metal urn has been decorated with 30 wired oranges and camellia leaves placed into a cone of 2.5-cm chicken wire filled with spagnum moss.

RIGHT A tri-coloured dogwood arrangement in green, red and black has been used to line a block of oasis in a 16-cm cube vase. Three rows of roses – 'Black Baccara, 'Jade' and 'Grand Prix' – have been arranged in straight lines to pick up the theme of the stripes of the dogwood.

LEFT A lightweight resin vase has been filled with kiwi vine to create a framework to arrange long stems of *Gloriosa rothschildiana*. The vase and arrangement have a natural empathy as they are both nearly see-through.

OPPOSITE BELOW A small cylinder vase has been filled with swirls of thin-stemmed Iranian dogwood and a hand-tied posy of 'Grand Prix' roses edged with galax leaves has been placed on the top.

more sculptural look and your eye is not so drawn to the two elements, the vase and the container. For many years we have been covering inexpensive plastic containers with double-sided tape and natural greenery such as leaves or herbs like rosemary and lavender, which still works very well for table arrangements, especially when the client wants to keep the arrangement and does not want the expense of the vase.

However, in my own home and for the vase majority of arrangements I prefer to use glass because it is so versatile and can be dressed up very easily with each passing season and be re-used again and again. Here these two vases have both used the same plant material in two very different ways. The round swirls of the Iranian dogwood suit the petalled dome of 'Grand Prix' roses, while the lines of three-coloured dogwood suit the geometric arrangement of the roses. Both containers are in empathy with the flower design and make up the overall effect.

small vases

I love to use small pots of flowers down a long table so you still have lots of room for large serving plates and it gives you a chance to use delicate small flowers. It also looks more casual and contemporary than one large long arrangement down the centre.

materials

5 old glass French yoghurt pots
40 stems of *Fritillaria olivieri*
50 stems of *Muscari armeniancum* 'Blue Spike'
10 stems of white *Rosa* 'Princess Spray'
50 stems of Lily of the Valley (*Convallaria majalis*)
a length of Ivy leaves (*Hedera Helix*)
a length of raffia

step by step

1 First tie two ivy leaves onto the sides of little yoghurt pot glasses with a length of raffia.

2 Fill with water mixed with flower food and then arrange little bunches of flower heads in your hand. Cut the spray roses up so you can use the individual heads. Trim the ends of each bunch to fit the pot.

large vase

If you are using a large glass vase you can use the natural structure of the stems to anchor your arrangements. The vase should be more than half the height of the flowers so if your lilies are 1 metre length I recommend a vase of 60 to 75cm. The average length of flower sold is generally around 60cm so it is a good idea to buy some containers ranging from 18cm up to 65cm for arranging flowers at home.

materials
6 stems of *Prunus serrulata* 'Pink Cloud'
1 flared glass vase 60cm tall
7 stems of oriental dark pink *Lillium* 'Mero Star'

step by step

1 Fill the vase with water mixed with flower food. The flower food acts as an antibacterial agent as well as a food for the flowers. It helps to keep the water clear and the flowers to have an enhanced life. First arrange the 6 branches of foliage in the vase, which will give you a structure which you can then place the lilies into.

2 Take all the lower foliage off the ends of the stems so that they are clean. It is important not to have foliage in the water so that it does not cause bacteria build-up. Pinch out the pollen from the centre of the lilies that are slightly open and add them to the vase.

a glass vase four ways

materials

a big tub of pink dried larkspur
a big tub of blue dried larkspur
a 16-cm cube glass vase
a larger U-shaped glass vase
some floral foam bindwire
30 stems of *Tulipa* 'First Class'
30 stems of *Tulipa* 'Gander
Rhapsody'
30 stems of tulipa 'Synaeda Blue'

By far the most used vases in my collection are small cubes or tank vases which I have in a number of sizes from 10 cm to 20 cm. They are extremely versatile and can be used with an inner vase liner so that fruit, sweets and sand can be used, or filled with floral foam that is concealed from the outside by using leaves, reeds and berries.

OPPOSITE TOP RIGHT
A glass cube arrangement, comprising:
8 lemons
2 blocks of yellow oasis
half a bunch of ivy berries (*Hedera helix*)
5 stems of white *Skimmia confusa* 'Kew Green'
5 stems of *Hypericum* 'Jade'
3 stems of Asclepia 'Moby Dick'
9 stems of *Rosa* 'Supergreen'
12 stems of *Rosa* 'Alexis'

OPPOSITE BOTTOM RIGHT
To achieve this multi-colored arrangement, you will need:
a large bag of jelly beans
a 16-cm glass cube with a tumbler packed inside
half a bunch of *Viburnum tinus* berries
5 stems of rosehips
5 stems of *Hypericum* 'Jade'
5 stems of white *Skimmia confusa* 'Kew Green'
5 stems of *Alchemilla mollis*
5 stems of *Rosa* 'Alexis'
5 stems of *Rosa* 'Supergreen'
5 stems of *Rosa* 'Milano'
5 stems of *Rosa* 'Beauty by Oger'
5 stems of *Rosa* 'Grand Prix'
5 stems of *Rosa* 'Milva'

RIGHT This stunning tall arrangement would suit a large event. To make it, use:
a 16-cm cube and a 12-cm cube
a bag of blue and a bag of white sand
15 stems of *Agapanthus* 'Donau'
half a bunch of flowering *Eucalyptus perriniana*

step by step

1 Place a layer of pink larkspur blossom at the base of the vase. Put the 16cm cube on top of the blossom and then add a layer of dark blue blossom and then a layer of pink blossom and carry on in stripes until you reach the top. Fill with water and flower food.

2 Strip all the tulips of their lower foliage and hand tie them into a spiral bunch by placing each stem at a 35 degree angle to the left of the previous one. Every 5 or 6 tulips twist the bunch in your hand so that you are working on all sides.

3 Trim the tulip stems and place into the central glass vase filled with water and flower food. Gently cut the tie to relax the tulips so that they move over the edge of the container.

flat container

Glass flat- and straight-sided containers are among my favourites because they allow you to customise your container in so many ways. Here I have used blond mikado reeds, a dried reed grown principally in South Africa. We also use equisetum in the same ways, as well as other green reeds. Exotic leaves with great markings are also effective for this sort of treatment, as well as thinly cut slices of citrus fruits such as oranges, lemons and limes.

materials

1 bunch of dried blonde mikado reed (*Ischyrolepsis hystrix*)
4 stems of *Rosa* 'Black Baccara'
8 stems of *Rosa* 'Bella Donna'
8 stems of *Rosa* 'Wow'
an oblong glass dish
a block of floral foam
a length of cord

step by step

1 Soak the floral foam until the bubbles cease to rise. Cut the floral foam to fill the base of the glass dish, leaving a centimetre around the edge. Cut the mikado reed to the same height as the glass dish to fill the gap between the edge and the foam. Cut the rose heads and place in the foam to create a neat line.

2 Continue across the dish with rows of different coloured roses. It is important to try to choose roses which have heads of a similar size so that it creates a very graphic arrangement. Edge with 4 bundles of mikado reed tied with matching cord.

spring arrangement

Glass containers are extremely versatile and also can be easily adapted to create many different designs. Two of my favourite liners for circular arrangements are dogwood and pussy willow. Both of these stems are very malleable in the spring when the sap is rising. These straight-sided bowls are very versatile as they can be used encased by floral foam as well as be decorated inside – see My Signature Style page 23 or Colour page 74. A 30-cm diameter bowl is my most popular.

materials

20 stems of pussy willow
(*Salix caprea*)
5 stems of *Viburnum opulus*
'Roseum'
a bunch of *Camellia japonica*
5 stems of *Hyacinthus orientalis*
'Annalisa'
10 stems of *Veronica* 'Dark Martje'
5 stems of lilac (*Syringa vulgaris*
'Dark Koster')
10 stems of *Anemone coronaria*
'Mona Lisa Blue'
10 stems of *Ranunculus ranobelle*
'Inra Wit'
10 stems of *Tulipa* 'Negritta'
q bunch of *Senecio greyii*
a bunch of ivy (*Hedera helix*)
a 30-cm straight-sided glass bowl
2 blocks of floral foam

step by step

1 Wind the pussy willow round the inside edge of the glass dish. Place one block of soaked oasis into the centre of the bowl and cut the other into two halves and place round the side so that it fits snugly and the oasis is a few centimetres above the edge of the glass container.

2 Green up the floral foam by using the small sprigs of the 3 varieties of the foliage, making sure they all radiate from the central point of the arrangement.

3 Next add the five stems of *Viburnum opulus* and lilac and then the more delicate spring flowers such as the hyacinths, tulips and veronica.

4 Finally add the anemones, placing them at different heights and depths throughout the arrangement.

a vegetative arrangement

Vegetative designs present floral material as they naturally grow so that the arrangement is mimicking nature. Very often in this style of arrangement the plant material is placed in groups. Stem placements may be parallel (upright) or radial (fan-shaped), with the stems arranged as they grow. If the flowers grew upright next to each other, as do liatris, gladioli and antirrhinums, you would arrange them in that way to depict a vegetative or naturalistic design. If they bend out, such as irises or strelitzias, they would be arranged in a more radial position.

materials

10 *Strelitzia reginae*
20 stems of contorted willow
50 stems of *Phormium tenax variegatum*
15 stems of *Leucospermum cordifolium* 'Coral'
10 stems of *Hypericum* 'Dolly Parton'
10 stems of *Rosa* 'Macarena'
10 stems of *Eustomia russellianum* 'King Violet'
a 20-cm glass cube
2 blocks of floral foam

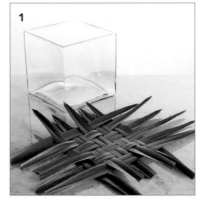

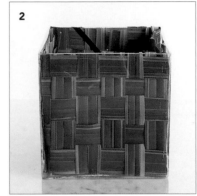

step by step

1 Lay out 6 stems of *Phormium tenax* horizontally and then weave another 6 stems vertically through, to create a basket-weave effect. If you find this difficult you can always use a staple gun to keep the bottom and top leaves in place.

2 Trim to fit neatly into the glass cube. Use some floral foam tape to keep it upright until you are ready to add the oasis. Pack out the floral foam so that the container is completely filled and make sure that the foam is at least 5cm above the edge of the container.

3 Add the willow throughout the arrangement and then green up the base with camellia followed by groups of leucospermums, roses, lisianthus and hypericum. Finally add the strelitzia so that they are all pointing outward from the centre of the arrangement.

creating a natural container

Using a plastic container you can create lots of natural bases for table arrangements. I like to create my own containers because it gives the end result a more sculptural effect. It can also be a very inexpensive way of concealing a simple plastic pot if you use dark glossy leaves such as aspidistra, laurel or rhododendron.

step by step

1 Place a length of double-sided tape around the plastic pot. I prefer to use the heavy duty carpet tape from DIY stores. Cut little bunches of heather from the plant and stick them to the double-sided tape.

2 Bend the heavy florists' wires into hair pins and tape onto the end of the candle.

3 To secure the heather, place a wire or a ribbon around the bowl. Fill the bowl with two blocks of soaked floral foam. Make sure that the foam is at least 2cm above the edge of the container by packing out the bottom with the ends of the block of foam. Trim the bottom of the wires on the candle and then place firmly in the centre of the foam so that the candle is well anchored.

4 Use the foliage to cover the floral foam, making sure that it all radiates from a central point. Use at least 3 different types of foliage to give an interesting textural effect.

5 Place the large headed flowers into the arrangement first at different heights and depths around the bowl. Next add the hypericum cut up into small sprigs. Use the roses in groups to balance with the larger heavy flowers. Add the white chrysanthemum 'White Revert.'

CLOCKWISE
A glass tumbler edged
with laurel leaves and filled
with a spring posy of
hellebores, tulips, spray
roses, skimmia, *Viburnum
opulus* and hyacinths.

A basket externally lined
with rosemary and blossom
filled with roses,
ranunculus, lilac and
Viburnum opulus.

Cut rosemary edges a
bowl filled with gloriosa,
'Milano' roses, yellow
ranunculus, yellow and
pink carnations, jade
hypericum, leucospermum
and ivy berries.

creating organic containers

The combination of fruit and vegetables mixed with flowers has for a long time been popular with flower arrangers. I love to use capsicums, Savoy cabbages, melons and pumpkins as containers scooped out and filled with foam or around other containers with glue, wire or double-sided tape in the case of asparagus, leeks and sugar cane. Round vegetables such as radicchio, turnips and aubergine work very well cut in half and scored so they fit on the edge of the bowl or wired around the container.

materials

10–15 globe artichokes
1 plastic pot
a length of aluminium wire
a roll of double-sided tape
a roll of pot tape
a block of floral foam
10 stems of green dill
5 stems of *Viburnum opulus* berries
a few stems of hebe
10 stems of dark dahlias
10 stems of *Rosa* 'Circus'
10 stems of red peonies

step by step

1 Cut the artichoke in half and clean out the choke. Thread onto aluminium wire until you have enough to go around the bowl. Tie the wire tightly round the bowl, twisting the ends.

2 Start placing your foliage into the arrangement beginning with the hebe and followed by the viburnum berries to give a loose feel.

3 Place your roses throughout the arrangement, followed by the peonies and fill in the gaps with the dahlias.

4 Complete the arrangement using the dill to achieve a soft finish.

ABOVE Three glass tumblers have been encircled by double-sided tape onto which I have attached spears of asparagus. Small posies of Cherry Brandy roses, green Prado carnations, *Alchemilla mollis* and *Asclepias* posies have been added into the vegetative tumblers.

RIGHT Aubergines have been cut into half and scored to sit on the top of a straight-sided plastic bowl. Moss has been added to the gaps and the vegetables have been secured with raffia In the centre floral foam has been added and the sprigs of *Viburnum tinus* blossom and small bunches of black grapes wired with a double mount have been placed around the arrangement, all radiating from the centre point. 'Nicole' and 'Aroma' roses have been placed into the arrangement with the brown 'Choco' mini gerberas.

basket arrangement

Baskets usually made from interwoven cane, rushes, wood or metal are used throughout the floral industry. Round baskets and arrangements are perfect for centrepieces for tables and are also extremely popular as gifts. All baskets need to be lined with plastic to hold either floral foam or water and chicken wire. For this delicate spring collection of flowers it is best to use chicken wire and water as it allows all the fragile stems to drink more freely than they can in floral foam. Many of the spring bulbs such as hyacinths, muscari, scillas and fragile flowers such as marguerite daises and forget-me-nots will last much longer if they are arranged in water rather than foam.

materials
a round grey basket
a round plastic pot
a length of chicken wire
a reel of florist wire
10 stems of *Tulipa* 'Blue Diamond'
5 stems of *Viburnum opulus*
'Roseum'
10 stems of *Scilla sibirica*
5 stems of lilac (*Syringa vulgaris*
'Dark Koster')
20 stems of *Myosotis*
10 stems of *Argyranthemum
frutescens*
a bunch of berried *Hedera helix*
a bunch of *Senecio greyii*

step by step

1 Fill the basket with a plastic liner and then add a foot of 5-cm chicken wire. Make sure that it fits snugly into the plastic pot and then attach with loops of wires to the basket so that it fits firmly. Fill the plastic container with water mixed with flower food.

2 For most of my designs a third of the plant material will be foliage and I usually like to select at least three different varieties to create a good base for the flowers. Start by adding the ivy, then the senecio and then the lime green blossom balls of the *Viburnum opulus*.

3 When the chicken wire is covered you can begin to add the flowers. It is best to start with the woody stemmed flowers such as the flowering lilac and the heavy bulb stems such as the scillas.

4 Then add the tulips, taking care to make sure that all the stems radiate from the central point and that each flower is represented throughout the arrangement at different heights and depths to create a natural effect. Finally add the delicate flowers such as the daisies and the forget-me-nots.

larger arrangements

When creating an impressive arrangement, take time to secure your mechanics and ensure your chicken wire or foam is well wired and taped. Secure the bucket inside the urn or container. Use the foliage to establish the outline. Remember to recess some of the plant material so that it draws they eye into the design, and keep it topped up with water.

materials

a stand and amphora
10 *Lillium* 'Sorbonne'
15 stems of *Paeonia* 'Red Charm'
10 stems of *Viburnum opulus* 'Roseum'
10 stems of flowering *Photina fraseri* 'Red Robin'
10 tall branches of *Sorbus aria* 'Majestica'
10 tall branches of *Prunus* 'Sato-zakura'
10 stems of *Antirrhinum majus* 'Potomac Rose'
5 white *Delphinium elatum* 'Snow Queen Arrow'
15 stems of Larkspur (*Delphinium consolida* 'Pink Perfection')
5 long branches of rhododendron
10 stems of long *Ruscus hypophyllium*
10 stems of lilac (*Syringa vulgaris* 'Dark Koster')
10 stems of weeping willow (*Salix babylonica*)
8 stems of solomon's seal (*Polygonatum*)
10 stems of *Moluccella laevis*

freestanding amphora

To create a really large arrangement it is best to choose flowers of many different shapes. Tall flowers give the arrangement height while star-shaped and round flowers help to give the arrangement body. Around a third of the arrangement will be made up of foliage and to create a really natural effect try to use at least five varieties. Pick some that are bushy, some that are tall and some that are trailing. All the plant material should give the impression that it radiates from one central point; the stems will not all actually radiate from the same point as this would lead to an awful lot of criss-crossing at one point.

step by step

1 Line the pot with a plastic bucket. Use some scrunched up chicken wire to enable the pot to sit flush with the container. Fill with water, mixed with flower food.

2 Using a mixture of the foliages create the outline of the arrangement you wish to create. For a large freestanding arrangement the flowers should be one and a half times the height of the container.

3 For a round arrangement all the stems should radiate from a central point. Once you have got a good base and structure with the foliage you can start to add the flowers, beginning with the prunus.

4 Use trailing foliages such as the ruscus, solomon's seal and willow to trail down over the front of the pot.

5 Next add all the woody stems such as the lilac and the viburnum and all the tall spires such as moluccella, antirrhinum, larkspur and delphinium.

6 Finally add the star-shaped lilies throughout the arrangement at different heights and depths and then place the peonies to fill out any gaps.

trailing top table arrangement

Trailing arrangements like this are useful for top table arrangements, conference tables or placing on mantelpieces. For a top table I use a low spray tray but for a mantel arrangement, particularly if the mantel isn't very deep, I prefer to use a trough such as a window box so you can place the floral foam blocks upright. This gives you more potential for filling with the container with water as well as allowing you to create a more substantial arrangement.

materials

10 stems of *Rosa* 'Vendella'
10 stems of *Rosa* 'Peach'
10 stem of peach spray rose
10 stems of *Lupinus* 'Little Eugenie'
10 stems of *Alchemilla mollis*
10 stems of *Panicum* 'Fountain'
10 stems of *Tulipa* 'Angelique'
7 stems of *Paeony lactiflora* 'Sorbet'
20 stems of *Polygonatum multiflorum*
1 long spray tray
2 blocks of floral foam
a reel of floral foam tape

step by step

1 Soak the two blocks of floral foam in water until the bubbles cease rising and then place the two blocks on a flat white spray tray and tape them down. Trim the corner of the oasis to help the placing of the material. It is always best to make this kind of arrangement in situ, so place the tray right at the front of the table and start to create the outline by using the trailing stems of solomon's seal.

2 Next add the fountain grass evenly throughout the design.

3 Fill out the design by using the *Alchemilla mollis* and *Viburnum opulus* and then place 7 of the lupins through the design as your longest flowers.

4 Using the spray roses and the standard roses fill out the design and then place the open peonies in the most prominent positions. These central flowers will be the area that the eye is drawn to, which is known as the focal point.

5 Fill any gaps with the astilbe, working from the trailing edge through to the edge of the foam on the other side. Athough these arrangements are often viewed from the front of the table make sure it also looks good from the back, which will be the view of the bride and groom and guests of honour sitting at the top table.

oval table decoration

The heaviness of ivy foliage in this arrangement gives it a very natural feel and makes this an oval mass design. If you wish to create a more horizontal feel to your arrangement use more stems parallel to the surface of the table. When the horizontal stems predominate, the arrangement is known as a horizontal design.

materials

a bunch of white *Ranunculus* 'Ranobelle Inra Wit'
5 stems of *Syringa vulgaris* 'Madame Florent Stepman'
a bunch of *Tulipa* 'Winterberg'
a bunch of *Hamamelis virginiana*
7 *Rosa* 'Alexis'
7 *Rosa* 'Avalanche'
5 stems of *Viburnum opulus*
a bunch of ivy trails (*Hedera helix*)
a bunch of fruiting ivy
a 30-cm long rectangular container
a tall pillar candle
2 blocks of floral foam
a roll of floral tape
2 green bamboo skewers

step by step

1 Soak two blocks of floral foam and arrange in the rectangular container so that the foam is at least 3cm above the edge of the container. Cut the green bamboo cane to create 4 legs and tape these onto the bottom of the candle. Press the candle down in the centre of the arrangement so that it is firmly anchored.

2 Next take the ivy trails and help establish the flowing outline of the arrangement using the longer pieces at either end of the arrangement. Use ivy berries to create a diamond-shaped base for your flowers.

3 Add branches of the witch hazel and the *Viburnum opulus* through the arrangement to create movement and to add interest.

4 Taking each individual flower, place through the centre of the arrangement at different heights and depths using a zig-zag motion from left to right. Fill in any gaps with sprigs of white lilac.

wirework

Traditionally speaking, wiring flowers was the preserve of the professional florist and separated them from the 'flower arrangers' who tended only to make arrangements. Wiring is used to reinforce in a visually unobtrusive manner weak or fragile stems to support the flower heads or to create floral items to be worn or carried. Principally, flowers are wired either to be worn, for small and large-scale decorative work or for hanging. Before the widespread use of floral foam wiring was much more prevalent because moss was primarily used, so it was necessary to wire flowers far more often. In fact, before foam wreath bases were invented all floral sympathy tributes were made this way. There are still a few florists and nurserymen who make these tributes in the traditional way, but sadly this skill is dying. Wiring flowers obviously is more labour intensive than arranging them in foam or hand tying, so it is more expensive and less economic.

The general rule for wiring is to use as light a wire as possible to do the job and then to keep it as neat as possible. Floristry wire comes in many gauges and lengths and you need to pick a wire to secure the flower or other plant material that is just strong enough and not too heavy so as to damage the flower or stem or make your work look too rigid and not natural enough. You have to be very careful also when handling the flower not to damage the petals by bruising, as this will quickly cause discoloration.

Wiring for weddings is generally delicate and somewhat complex and requires patience. Wiring for large-scale decoration or for the Christmas period is very hard on your hands and nails. Two further reasons why wiring flowers and plant materials does not suit all wannabe florists!

RIGHT Large heads of pink cymbidium have been wired into a posy and the handle of wires has been covered with a matching silk ribbon.

buttonholes

Buttonholes are wired flowers with leaves that are designed to be worn on the lapel. In the United Kingdom we call a collection of flowers and leaves to be worn like this a corsage or spray but in America it is know as a boutonniere. Generally speaking a buttonhole can be made form any type of flower, but there are some that are far more popular because they are inexpensive and wire well. Carnations and roses are particularly popular as they do last very well; orchids are very successful too but tend to be more expensive to purchase. Small germini gerberas, mini-sunflowers, ranunculus, smaller calla lilies and even daisies, cornflowers and stephanotis are among the flowers we are regularly asked for.

materials

a sprig of rosemary
a branch of *Viburnum tinus*
a *Rosa* 'Alexis'
a branch of *Hedera helix*
a length of Paraffilm
some 0.71mm wires
some 0.28mm or 0.32mm wires

CLOCKWISE FROM TOP LEFT Green *Cymbidium* orchid edged with camellia leaves; speckled *Phalaenopsis* orchid with lily grass loops and camellia leaves; carnation with lime hypericum; Hebe and gloriosa with grass loops and a binding of decorative pink floral wire.

step by step

1 Select a well-formed rose and remove the stem just below the seedbox. Insert a short 0.71mm stub wire into the stem and up into the seedbox. Double leg mount three sprigs of rosemary and two sprigs of *Viburnum tinus* flowers. To create a double leg mount make a hairpin bend with the wire and loop one wire over the over three times. Choose three good ivy leaves and stitch through the vein at the back of the leaf and take one leg over the other.

2 Take a reel of Paraffilm and stretch it so that you bind the wires together. This helps to keep the moisture in and softens the wires. Arrange three pieces of rosemary around the rosehead and the two sprigs of *Viburnum tinus* berries and then edge with the three ivy leaves. Bind them all together with the Paraffilm and then trim the stem so that it is about 3.5cm long. Add a pearl-headed pin so that the buttonhole can be secured onto clothing.

ABOVE Corsage of two cymbidium heads with jasmine and gardenia leaf. This is a beautiful combination, both long lasting and fragrant!

RIGHT A simple garland of margarite daisies threaded through their stem and the centre of their flower head.

ABOVE For a last-minute touch for a wedding you can reel wire flower garlands and heads onto a trug and add petals. Here we have used clematis, snakeshead fritillarias and 'Aroma' rose petals.

RIGHT This bridesmaid's hoop has been simply bound with ivy and then covered with clematis and bunches of brodiaea and cornflowers. Wired heads of hydrangea have been added through the ring.

wired accessories

Wired accessories are generally made for celebrations, wedding in particular. Baskets and bridesmaids' rings are simply bound and, as fragile blooms have been used, they need to be made at the last minute and will only last for the duration of the ceremony. If you require wired flowers to last for the whole day you

need to wire each indvidual flower head and leaf and chose long-lasting varieties such as roses, orchids, gypsophila and good drying flowers such as lavender, eryngium, echinops, statice, limonium and helichrysum. As an alternative, I would advocate last minute wiring with simple binding wire as long as the bearer has been warned of the short life expectancy of the design. The napkin rings on these pages have been created by wiring flower heads onto either a decorative florists wire or a delicate silver wire.

1

materials

a reel of purple florists' wire
a thin 3–5mm reel of ribbon
a stem of *Hyacinthus orientalis*
'Minos'

step by step

1 Pull the individual pips off the hyacinth and thread tham onto the length of purple wire so that they are all facing the same direction.

2 When you have completed enough to bind the napkin loop the two wires together and trim with a 3-looped ribbon bow.

bridal headdress

Wearing a ring of flowers dates from ancient Greece, and it is still the most popular floral accessory for brides and their attendants. The choice of flowers and headdress will be influenced by how the bride will be wearing her hair and whether or not she chooses to wear a veil. It should be planned to tie in with the bridal bouquet.

materials

a head of *Hydrangea macrophylla* 'Mein Liebling'
a stem of *Helleborus orientalis*
2 stems of everlasting sweet pea (*Lathyrus latifolius* 'Albus')
2 stems of flowering *Eucalyptus perriniana*
5 stems of *Rosa* 'Mimi Eden'
a selection of silver wires
a roll of green Paraffilm
a selection of fine wires – 0.28mm and 0.32mm
an Alice band

step by step

1 The size, shape and structure of the flowers and foliage will determine which wiring technique is required. As long as the method works and the wire gauge is correct for the purpose and all the visible wires are concealed, it does not really matter how this has been achieved. The eucalyptus leaves used in this headdress have been wired with a double leg mount. To create one of these take a silver wire, make a hairpin bend and then fold one wire over the other 3 times. The same method has been used for the flowering eucalyptus. The everlasting sweetpea and hydrangea have been wired by taking a few florets and placing a wire through the fleshy part of the stem and then looping one wire over the other 3 times. The rose and the hellebores have been wired by placing a wire through the base of the flower head. To do this you put a silver wire into the calyx, carefully twist round the base of the calyx and then bring it down the stem, looping one wire over the other 3 times in all.

2 When you have wired all the flower heads, florets and leaves, tape them with floral tape. (Floral tape is a plastic or rubbery tape, of which there are several types. I use Paraffilm, which is a trade name for a narrow thin plastic tape composed of paraffin and polyilofelin.)

3 Take the plastic Alice band and cover it with the Paraffilm. This will make it easier to tape on your wires and it also gives the Alice band a natural green colour.

Starting with the eucalyptus leaf at the end, bind individual flowers to the plastic alice band by stretching the Paraffilm. Alternate each flower, working across each side of the alice band and edging with the leaves. Continue all the way across until you have reached the other side.

All-round floral headdresses or circlets are made by creating a round floral frame by overlapping two 0.71mm wires and overlapping them with another two 0.71mm wires, binding them together with 0.20mm silver wire and then creating a round circlet with two hooks to fit the size desired. Individual wired and gutted flower heads are then taped onto the frame in the same way as for an alice band.

LEFT A round wreath to be worn on the crown of the head has been made from variegated ivy leaves, pips of tuberosa, pink ranunculus and muscari.

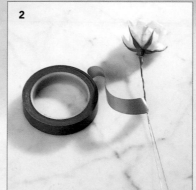

seasonal wreath

materials

a 35-cm wire wreath frame
a bag of sphagnum moss
a bunch of Ivy berries (*Hedera helix*)
a bunch of blue pine (*Pinus wallichiana*)
a bunch of Scots pine (*Pinus sylvestris*)
a bunch of *Skimmia japonica* 'Rubinetta"
a bunch of holly berries (*Ilex aquifolium* 'Madam Briot'
a length of silver ribbon
a reel of silver cord
a strong pair of scissors
a reel of florist's wire (0.56mm)
one 0.90mm stub wire

Throughout the world in all cultures, rings and wreaths of fresh or dried plant materials have traditionally been used as a symbol of eternity and hospitality and this remains a significant gesture today. Wreaths that are used to decorate a door are constructed on a mossed base which is a better foundation than floral foam. Foam only works for flower heads and for temporary or short celebrations. To most wreaths, heavy decorations and embellishments such as cones and fruits are added which need to be well anchored into the moss to survive the festive period.

OPPOSITE A large open floral foam heart frame has been edged with ivy trails wired into the base and then topped with a mass of multicoloured roses. Trails of ivy and muehlenbeckia vines have then been added on top of the flowers to give a more natural feel, Wired faux butterflies have been wired into the design.

step by step

1 Wind the end of the reel of wire onto the inner frame of the wreath ring. Meanwhile tease apart the spagnum moss removing any branches, leaves, cones or other foreign bodies. Place several handfuls of moss about 5cm high on the frame and bind the moss on firmly. Continue adding moss evenly and binding diagonally across the frame until it is completely covered with moss. Once completed, bind the reelwire around the frame for a second time and ensure the density of the moss is even throughout. Cut the wire and place the end into the moss and, taking a pair of floristry scissors, trim off any straggly pieces of moss.

2 Attach the reel wire again to the edge of the frame and then start to bind on bunches of cut foliage about 3 – 4 cm long. To create a good binding, trim the lower stem of additional foliage. Carry on around the ring in an anti-clockwise fashion using groups of foliage.

3 Repeat the pattern of foliage until you have created a lovely variegated ring that has lots of different textures as well as colours within it.

4 When you have completed the ring, push a pair of scissors through the back of the frame and ease in the cord to attach the wreath to a doorway.

5 Create three loops of ribbon and wire through the centre with a 0.90mm wire and then pin into the base of the frame.

topiary candelabra

Every decorating florist needs a good set of sturdy metal table candelabras that can be dressed up for any season or event. I love the effect of covering the metal stems and arms with plant material so that the candelabra become more of a topiary form than candelabra. Hebe, rosemary, ivy, box and eucalyptus are among my favourites, and in winter, I love to use dogwood, berried cotoneaster, contorted willow and spruce. For spring, pussy willow and blossom are effective, as well as catkin-laden birch. For any season equisetum works well, as does this painted birch, which I buy dipped in paint but you could spray paint if you do not have access to supplies of painted birch.

materials

a metal 5-prong candelabra
a 50-cm floral foam wreath
2 bunches of painted birch twigs
a reel of heavy blue wire
5 taper candles
a block of floral foam
a roll of pot tape
5 stems of hydrangea
15 stems of *Eustoma russellium*
'Fuji Silver Blue'
7 stems of *Agapanthus* 'Atlantic
Ocean'
32 stems of *Rosa* 'Sterling Silver'
10 stems of stock (*Mathiola incana*
'Centum Lavender')
a bunch of *Senecio greyii*
a bunch of berried ivy Hedera helix
a bunch of *Hebe albicans* 'Red Edge'

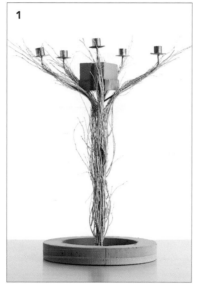

step by step

1 Bind the stem of the candlestick with the birch twigs using the reel wire. Place the soaked floral foam into the centre of the candlestick and tape it into place. Soak the floral ring and stand around the base of the candlestick. Trim off the edge of the foam to make it easier to add the plant material. Paring a little off the edge and smoothing the shape is sometimes referred to as chamfering.

2 Place the ivy in the floral foam working from all angles to create a loose shape, including some trails down the candlestick. Fill in with senecio and hebe to give you a good outline and shape. Fill the ring with foliage all around so that you cover the floral foam ring.

3 Starting with the largest flowers position the hydrangea flower heads around the candelabra. For the top arrangement you should be aiming for a ball shape. Continue to build the shape with the agapanthus, stocks, and lisianthus. Finally place your roses in pairs throughout the arrangement. Repeat the process with the remaining flowers to fill up the floral foam ring at the base of the arrangement.

4 Finally place your roses in pairs throughout the arrangement and complete by placing in your candles. Secure the base of the candles in the candelabra with floral tac.

RIGHT A single-stemmed candelabra has been covered with hebe with binding wire and then wired 'Avalanche' roses and cream 'Gracia' spray roses have been wired and placed into the greenery.

wired fruit basket

Using fruit and vegetables has been a trademark of my designs for two decades. I often get inspiration from the fruit and vegetable market with all the lovely textures and colours of the produce particularly when flowers are more expensive and scarce in the autumn and winter time. This basket arrangement has been perennially popular either in the summer with green apples and pastel summer flowers or in the autumn and winter with red apples and dramatic colour combinations.

materials

a strong sturdy basket
a plastic wellbeck bowl
4 blocks of green floral foam
30 Washington red apples
sphagnum moss
5 stems of American oak (*Quercus palustris*)
1 bunch of ivy berries (*Hedera helix*)
10 stems of red *Skimmia japonica* 'Rubella'
5 stems of golden holly berries (*Ilex aquifolium* 'Golden Verboom')
10 stems of *Rudbeckia hirta*
7 stems of *Leucospermum cordiolium* 'Succession'
15 *Rosa* 'Ruby Red'
15 *Rosa* 'Acqua'

step by step

1 Wire up the 30 apples by pushing an 0.90mm florists wire through the lower half of the fruit so that an equal amount protrudes from each side. Then place a second wire in the other direction of the lower part of the fruit and then twist all 4 wires together leaving 2 wire stems which can be used to attach the apple to the basket frame.

2 Starting with the bottom layer attach 15 apples around the edge of the basket. When you have completed the bottom tier wire the second layer into the basket frame.

3 Then fill a large plastic liner with 4 blocks of soaked floral foam. Secure into the liner with pot tape and then fit snugly into the basket by placing sphagnum moss all around. Make sure that the floral foam is at least 5cm above the edge of the container so that you can create a rounded effect.

4 Starting with the ivy berries, trim into branches of about 8cm and place all around the basket at different heights, but all radiating from a central point. Then follow with the skimmia and American oak until you can hardly see the floral foam. By now you should have created a lovely rounded structure into which you can put your flowers.

5 First cut the ilex berries into branches of 8–10cm and place these around the arrangement, and then add the leucospermums and the textural rudbeckia. Finally add the roses in groups of threes.

conical topiary

Conical or geometric-shaped arrangements are usually created for celebrations. By using chicken wire and moss you can construct much larger arrangements with more densely packed flowers than you can do using floral foam. It also allows you to create any size of arrangement you wish. For a corporate event in an enormous atrium we have made arrangements as large as 6 metres tall. The larger the topiary required the more sophisticated the structure or mechanics have to be.

materials

a metal urn
a conical topiary frame
50cm of 2-cm chicken wire
a bale of sphagnum moss
a reel of heavy florists' wire
a selection of wires
5 bunches of *Narcissi tazetta* 'Laurens Koster'
5 bunches of orange *Ranuculus* 'Ranobelle Inra Zalm'
50 stems of yellow *Calendula officianalis* 'Greenheart Orange'
50 stems of *Rosa* 'Lemonade'
50 stems of *Rosa* 'Milva'
10 stems of *Forsythia intermedia* 'Spectabilis'
2 bunches of *Camellia japonica*
30 sharon fruit
30 stems of *Leucospermum cordifolium* 'Fireball'

step by step

1 Line the cone in chicken wire and then stuff it with sphagnum moss so that it is very firm.

2 Using the reel wire bind the chicken wire onto the frame and then wire it into the iron urn so that it is very stable.

3 Cover the frame with small sprigs of camellia foliage placed into the moss. Then arrange the 10 stems of forsythia into the bottom of the urn and place vertically around the frame so that they all meet at the top. Secure them with hairpin bends of heavy stub wire.

4 Next prepare all your flowers. Wire them by placing a heavy stub wire up the stem and into the flower head. Place two wires through the sharon fruit and then twist them together at the base.

5 Place the sharon fruit into the moss, evenly spaced. Add all the wired flowers, placing the narcissi last as they are the most delicate.

part three

celebrations

One of the greatest joys of working as a florist is that you get the chance
to create beautiful flowers for all the occasions that mark one's life. In
the main these are celebratory and even when sadly they mark a death
or are for remembrance, the sentiment expressed through the flowers is
to celebrate life. Flowers lighten our senses and enhance any event.
Whichever floral decorations you choose and however you achieve your
design, your flowers will be central to the occasion and will symbolize
the hope and love of your celebrations.

decorating your space

The choice of flowers, hardware and scale will all be determined by the space which you have to decorate and of course the budget. It is the skill of a good florist to make the most of the flowers whatever the budget so that they really get noticed and have the greatest impact. The type of occasion and event will also determine the choice.

In domestic situations there is normally one favoured place or several areas where you like to display your flowers. Most people select their flowers on the criteria of their space or their favourite vases. They have areas in their homes that have the most impact and choose their flowers on that basis.

For a large drinks party where everyone will mainly be standing, a large tall central arrangement will be more visible than lots of smaller vases. If the hall is very big as well as tall I often use a number of metre-high vases on occasional tables filled with orchids and tall papyrus to spread the colour and flowers throughout the party. A grand hall will also demand a more dramatic tall display where either large pedestals or topiary forms will be

needed to suit the scale. In a cathedral, two large urns and plinths on either side of the altar make more visual impact than decorating lots of pew ends.

The larger the venue the more hardware you will require and possibly greater planning as you may need to hire equipment to make your creations such as ladders and 'cherry pickers' and larger vans to transport the frames, mechanics and hardware, as well as the flowers. Working on site like this also requires public liability insurance and many venues and banqueting suites have specific rules and contracts governing who can work on their events. Always check first with the banqueting manager and take as much protection in the form of dustsheets and plastic liners and make sure you have all the materials you need for cleaning up after you have finished your work. It is also important to talk to the banqueting co-ordinator or wedding planner so that you are given an appropriate time slot to arrive so that you can dress the clothed tables. It is advisable to be there before the lighting engineers as they will be enhancing your

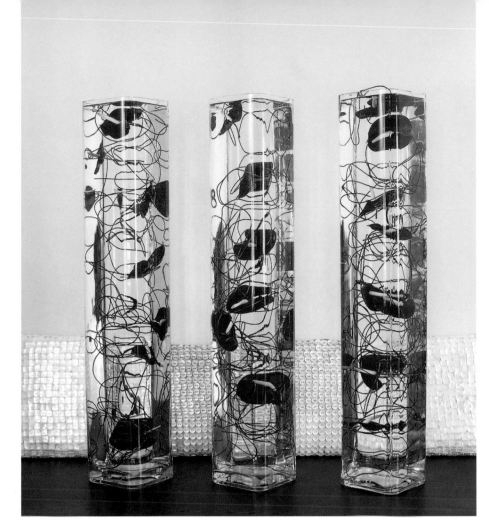

LEFT Three vases have been filled with anthurium heads suspended by gold aluminium wire. It is best to build this up from the bottom of the vase to the top and then fill with water to keep the flowers from floating to the top. The aluminium wire holds them in place when water is added. They last up to a week before becoming transparent.

OPPOSITE LEFT Asymmetrical arrangements grouped together have been popular now for a few years. Here again part of the interest lies in having oversized vases and then filling them with aluminium wire to keep the flowers in place. The long stemmed calla lilies have been bunched with swirls of wires to keep the flower heads in place. The effect makes a strong impact.

displays once they are in place and all the tables are dressed. Floral designers sometimes work as party planners and select the other contractors they work with and are responsible for the whole design. More often they liase with party planners and caterers, each adding their expertise to make the event truly special.

For traditional and country venues, wilder and more classical styles of arrangements work better than minimal geometric designs. A stark, modern venue may be perfect for the current vogue of minimal displays but it rarely works well if the scale of building is too vast as these type of arrangements get lost. Often this style of arranging is minimal on flowers but very heavy on hardware, requiring expensive large vases and plinths, not to mention very good lighting. Glass vases with suspended flowers look fantastic if 'up lit' and you get a lot of impact with not very many flowers so this is very economical on perishable products.

Whatever style you work in, every florist needs to have a good selection of hardware to create well-balanced creative floral displays and very often for the event florist it soon means you have a warehouse of accoutrements to flower arranging so that you can work in any style of building and for any kind of event!

There are so many ways to decorate a space, which is why there are so many different techniques to learn. Arches are great for church doorways for wedding ceremonies and they also provide the perfect canopy under which the bride and groom can be married. Depending on whether they are free standing or placed against a wall will determine what kind of mechanics you require and how it may be constructed. Some churches have perfect pews for decorating while others have replaced their original pews or are modern and have chairs which do not suit floral decorations so easily. For a traditional christening, the emphasis will be on decorating the font area of a church.

Marquees literally offer a blank canvas and are among my favourite to decorate. They are large spaces but can be inexpensively decorated by hiring topiary from garden nurseries and by adding just one or two really stunning displays. For any large venue I prefer to use low table decorations to spread the colour throughout the marquee.

Finally, using seasonal flowers will always be the best way of making use of a budget and it is always a good idea to bear in mind the budget and the scale when ordering your flowers. The directory section on pages 186–189 will help you make your selections.

One long flower trough makes a perfect container for a large flower display such as this. I have a set of long baskets with zinc liners but I often use a terracotta flower trough with a plastic liner and fill it with upright blocks of floral foam to give me lots of room to place a lot of front-facing and downward proportion plant material. For this early summer mantelpiece arrangement I have chosen gerberas, *Viburnum opulous*, *Euphorbia fulgens*, cymbidium orchids, leucospermum, and 'Calmia', 'Beauty by Oger' and 'Luxor' roses mixed with trailing ivies, solomon's seal and white leaf foliages.

OPPOSITE For my own home at Christmas I often choose to spray trays filled with foam and decorate two sides of the mantelpiece just using variegated foliages and a few thick pillar candles. It is amazing how long a simple foliage arrangement lasts. Ivy, holly, photinia and senecio look very festive with just a few wired ribbon bows. The suspended wreath is made from dried pomegranates glued onto a straw frame. The arrangements shown here are classical designs but you can just as easily create a more contemporary look by placing groups of vases with candles or votives.

Mantelpieces are great locations for flower arrangements because they place the flowers at eye level and give a spectacular display, taking up very little room.

LEFT A birthday cake arrangement designed on a round 'posy pad' of foam. The base has been covered with asparagus fern, camellia and the lime green balls are *Asclepias* 'Moby Dick'. The main flowers are pink ranunculus and 'Cherry Brandy' roses. The soft pink starry astrantia brings the taper candle colour through the arrangement.

The summer months are a great time for using bright colours as the light levels are higher and it suits the mood. The use of colour is very connected to the seasons and while hot climates such as India and Mexico are mad for colour, I had not discerned any link with food until, during a long discussion with my German friend and master florist Gregor Lersch, he observed that our 'taste' in floristry is not so dissimilar to our native diet. Northern European food is more bland than the spicy cusines of South America and Asia. In Northern Europe paler colours are more prevalent with an emphasis on neuturals. To this day I would say that the refined English taste is still to choose all white in the home, as it is deemed 'tasteful'. I doubt very much that a Chinese, Asian or South American would see the value of white in the same way!

ABOVE 'Cherry Brandy', 'Jade' and 'Aqua' roses have been hand tied with lime green 'Revert' chrysanthemums and orange leucospermum in the lime orange and pink colour mix. Orange kumquats conceal the stems in a cube vase.

LEFT The swirls of the fabric have been continued through this design, using roses and kumquats, which have been threaded onto a heavy florist wire. The muehlenbeckia vine adds a natural touch to the vibrancy of the flowers.

OPPOSITE The colours of the table runner have been mirrored in the flower designs and tableware. Three square dishes contain brightly coloured roses and kumquats. Deep red vanda orchids are dotted along the muehlenbeckia vine.

Outdoor parties require flowers that are natural and wild and suit the environment in which they are going to be seen. Ideally, garden parties should reflect the planting in the garden and therefore suit a more mixed composition. Seasonal flowers are therefore usually my choice; in spring I use bulb or tuber flowers such as tulips or ranunculus; later in the year I go for blossom, lilacs and early peonies, and in summer I love to use lavender, garden roses and sweet peas. For late summer I opt for the richer palettes of dark red dahlias, bright golden sunflowers and tall lilies.

ABOVE Pinks, oranges and lilacs have been made more vibrant with the use of *Alchemilla mollis* and the textual grey foliage *Senecio greyii*. Low flower arrangements allow you to talk across the table and I always like to choose some flowers that are scented when arranging flowers in the garden. Sweet peas are one of my favourite flowers to grow in my garden and are often used in my work.

LEFT Here in my own garden I have selected the flowers to tone with my fabrics on the table and seat pads. The selection of linen is a key role of the florist because it provides an important backdrop for your floral designs.

OPPOSITE For the table I have used two long spray trays surrounded by brightly coloured silk lanterns. An external pedestal arrangement is used as a focal point beyond the floral arch. This draws the eye beyond the table. Paper butterflies have been used throughout the garden, adding a colourful and delicate touch to the whole *al fresco* ensemble.

OPPOSITE Buffet table set for a celebratory afternoon tea. Foam rings around storm lanterns make perfect centrepieces for an informal table setting. As the rings and storm lanterns are large, I have chosen to use large headed flowers such as the white dill, pink lilies and also the large heads of peonies. A floral cake decoration has been designed using smaller headed flowers such as pink ranunculus and astrantia.

TOP LEFT The growth in lifestyle accessories has led to a huge increase in the accoutrements to the floral trade. Bright pink hanging votives add some colour to an ancient apple tree.

TOP RIGHT Scented lilies nestle among some white dill. Certain scents bring back memories and I love the musky scent of lilies because it takes me back to my own wedding day!

MIDDLE LEFT Napkin are tied with organza bows and faux butterflies.

MIDDLE RIGHT Fashions come and go but pink remain a favourite and ranunculus remain my very favourite flowers.

BOTTOM LEFT The dill gives these other showy flowers such as the lilies and dahlias a more country feel.

BOTTOM RIGHT Floral cake decorations are easy to make. I usually use a small piece of floral foam in the cut-off base of a white polystyrene cup. This one is filled here with flowering weigelia, ranunculus, roses and astrantia.

Long tables often require a series of vases down the centre. When entertaining at home I prefer to have several vases in a repeat sequence along the table so that I also have room for large plates and servers. With several vases the eye moves along the table and the flowers should be high enough to give a good floral presence but not so high that the guests cannot see one another. There are many vases available now that are around 16 to 20 cm high which is just perfect for a table centre. The most popular colour schemes are still white and green with a touch of colour and the colour schemes on these pages continue to be classical favourites each year, whatever the current floral vogue is.

LEFT Pale pink peonies, dahlias and sweet peas have been mixed with *Alchemilla mollis*, hydrangea, and vines of clematis montana. The frosted pink vases are perfectly toned for the flowers and the table runner.

TOP LEFT Napkin flowers are a lovely way of bringing the colour of the flowers across the table. Here forget-me-nots, hellebores, and spring blossom make a very pretty spring touch to the table.

LEFT One way of keeping a lovely napkin posy alive is to arrange the flowers in a plastic phial of water, covered with a leaf tied with raffia. Here blossom, catkins, ranunculus, hellebores and eryngium are all able to stay fresh. At the end of the meal, guests may like to have the individual posy as a keepsake to remind them of the occasion.

ABOVE I have always loved to use leeks in my arrangements because I love the graduation of colour from the the roots on the bottom to the lush green stems of the vegetables. Baby leeks have been placed around a small glass cylinder and then filled with a hand tied bouquet of *Viburnum opulous*, *Alchemilla mollis* white peonies and 'Renate' roses.

ABOVE LEFT A posy of hand tied gypsophila and 'Vendelle roses'. The soft coloured 'Vendelle' rose tends to go very well with ivory coloured fabric which is often chosen by brides in preference to white as it is more flattering.

ABOVE MIDDLE Some flower heads are so beautiful they are best admired on their own. These eucharis lilies are a very pure white with lovely lime green centres.

ABOVE RIGHT Hydrangea, peonies and gypsophila arranged in their own frosted vases.

MIDDLE LEFT Beautiful polished shells add to the glamour of the day and embellish the table decorations. Small shells have been cut to hold place name cards.

LEFT Delicate eucharist lilies and gypsophila in frosted vases provide a sumptuous display.

I love to use several different heights and shapes of vases made in the same material. Here frosted vases of different heights have been used to decorate an ivory and gold wedding table. The simple use of several different vases of all one type of flower gives a sumptuous look. The peony chair backs are tied with organza ribbon and on the side table there are vases of white 'flocked' sumata twigs, white massed hydrangea and white everlasting sweet pea. A floral lei of Singapore orchids links with a trio of tall frosted vases.

flower directory

The flower trade is so international and on such a huge global scale of production that seasonality of flowers is no longer such an important issue for the floral designer. However, I have to say that flowers that are still only available in their season and are therefore slightly rarer are the ones I treasure, more than ones I can buy any week of the year. Below is a list of some of our most used and favourite seasonal flowers and foliages by their most commonly known name in the flower trade.

early spring

1 Tulip
2 Anemone
3 Ranunculus
4 Hyacinth
5 Hellebore
6 Ivy
7 Lilac
8 Snowdrop
9 Daffodil
10 Hippeastrum (also called amaryllis)
11 Almond blossom
12 Cherry blossom
13 Myrtle
14 Magnolia
15 Skimmia
16 Snowberry
17 Flame euphorbia
18 Freesia
19 Forsythia
20 Pussy willow

mid spring

1 Narcissus
2 Forget-me-not
3 Grape hyacinth
4 Hyaciinth
5 Iris
6 Violet
7 Arum lily (also called calla lily)
8 Poppy
9 Mimosa
10 Forsythia
11 Catkin
12 Pussy willow
13 Tuberose
14 Ranunculus
15 Crown Imperial
16 Hellebore
17 Tulip
18 Prunus
19 Solomon's seal
20 Camellia

late spring

1 Guelder rose
2 Lilac
3 Bluebell
4 Lily-of-the-Valley
5 Freesia
6 Campanula
7 Wallflower
8 Sweet pea
9 Ranunculus
10 Euphorbia
11 Snake's head fritillary
12 Broom
13 Moluccella
14 Red hot poker
15 Iris
16 Ixia
17 Tulip
18 Godetia
19 Spiraea
20 Trollius

FROM TOP LEFT:
Hyacinthus orientalis
'Delt Blue'/white *Muscari*
and *Narcissus tazetta*
'Avalanche'/*Tulipa*
'Gander Rhapsody' and
Tulipa 'Synaeda Blue'

early summer

mid summer

late summer

FROM TOP RIGHT:
Paeonia lactiflora
'Karl Rosenfield'/*Rosa*
'Grand Prix,' *Rosa* 'Milano,'
Rosa 'Acqua'/*Dahlia*
'Arabian Night'

early autumn

1 Amaranthus
2 Cotinus
3 Snowberry
4 Bullrush
5 Blackberry
6 Dahlia
7 Curcuma
8 Belladonna lily
9 Scabious seed heads
10 Allium
11 Rudbeckia
12 Dill
13 Lipstick reed
14 Millet
15 Bupleurum
16 Asclepias
17 Aster
18 Pistachio
19 Chinese lantern
20 Miscanthus

mid autumn

1 Chili
2 Crab apple
3 Hypericum
4 Blackberry
5 Leucospermum
6 Arum lily (also called calla lily)
7 Chrysanthemum
8 Photinia
9 Lotus seed heads
10 American oak leaves
11 Beech
12 Callicarpa
13 Gourds
14 Cotinus
15 Red hot poker
16 Asclepias
17 Sunflower
18 Dogwood stems
19 Hypericum
20 Rattlesnake ginger

late autumn

1 Ornamental cabbage
2 Kangaroo paw
3 Crab apple
4 Leucodendron
5 Gourd
6 Chinese lantern
7 Holly berries
8 Hop
9 Flame euphorbia
10 Solidago
11 Rudbeckia
12 Shampoo ginger
13 Chincherinchee
14 Helconia
15 Hanging helconia
16 Water lily
17 Nerine
18 Limonium
19 Ligustrum berries
20 Amaranthus

FROM TOP LEFT:
Helianthus annus
'Flame'/*Ilex aquilfolium*
'Golden Verboon'/
Crysanthemum
'Tom Pearce'

early winter

1 Globe thistle
2 Helconia
3 Witch hazel
4 Protea
5 Bird of paradise
6 Queen protea
7 King protea
8 Galax leaves
9 Trachelium
10 Dogwood stems
11 Chrysanthemum
12 Skimmia
13 Grevillea
14 Ginger lily
15 Ornamental pineapple
16 Craspedia
17 Cotoneaster berries
18 Ligustrum berries
19 Crab apples
20 Lichen branches

midwinter

1 Photinia
2 Mistletoe
3 Tulip
4 Vanda orchid
5 Hippeastrum (also called amaryllis)
6 Eucalyptus seed pods
7 Ivy
8 Blue pine
9 Willow
10 Hypericum
11 Blueberry
12 Cymbidium orchid
13 Dendrobium orchid
14 Holly
15 Holly berries
16 Box
17 Anthurium
18 Pinus stobus
19 Oncidium orchid'
20 Mahonia

late winter

1 Peace lily
2 Snowflake
3 Brunia
4 Hippeastrum (also called amaryllis)
5 Carthamus
6 Arum lily (also called calla lily)
7 Broom
8 Heather
9 Silver kochia
10 Tulip
11 Anemone
12 Ranunculus
13 Brassica
14 Phalenopsis orchid
15 Slipper orchid
16 Banksia
17 Hibiscus
18 Cotton
19 Larch
20 Laurel

FROM TOP RIGHT:
Hippeastrum 'Mont Blanc/
Helleborus orientalis
'Trotter's Spotted'/
Leucojum 'Spring
Snowflake'

index

acknowledgements

To produce any illustrated book there is a large team who work together very hard and often over a long period of time to achieve the end result. This stunning book has been no exception and I have had the privilege to work with many dedicated people who were prepared to contribute their many talents (and go that extra mile) to make this book so special and who have also been great fun to work with. It was my great pleasure to work with Sian Irvine who has produced all the stunning photography. These wonderful images have enhanced my work and have been beautifully designed into this book by the designer Maggie Town. I like to have a little flexibility on what I may produce each 'shoot' day depending on what inspires me at the flower market and this can start to be a little of a headache and then just enormously annoying when you are trying to lay out a book. Maggie has been amazingly tolerant and done a really wonderful job! As usual I have a long suffering editor who has had to cajole, coax and encourage some text out of me and I am particularly grateful to Kate John for her sympathetic yet firm approach.

Over the years I have had the pleasure to work with some very talented florists and at present I have a very special staff, many of whom have been with me a long time. Sarah Jackson has been brilliant in cheerfully organising the day-to-day running of my business, and has contributed enormously to the creativity of this book, along with Rachel Mashiter, Samantha Griffiths and Anita Everard, who work on special events, weddings and at The Flower School. To the rest of the Paula Pryke Flower team based at The Flower House: Ann, Tania, Gina, Jo, Anne, Penny and Jis Sook, thank you; Chris and Anna, thank you for doing such a wonderful job at Liberty with Hisako, Monica, Mira and Angela; Anita and Natasha, and all the great team outside The Conran Shop at Brompton Cross, thank you. Thanks also to all my fantastic (long standing and long suffering) suppliers, particularly Dennis Edwards, Marcel Van Eijsden and Kees Ross, who supply the lovely flowers and have supported and encouraged me enormously in my flower enterprises.

And thanks to all my clients!

For details of the Paula Pryke Flower School, please contact:
The Flower School, Cynthia Street, London N1 9JF, UNITED KINGDOM.
Tel: (44) 20 77837 7373   Website: www.paula-pryke-flowers.com